• Obscenity & the Arts •

Anthony Burgess

Germaine Greer

Andrew Biswell

The Context of Obscenity & The Arts
Copyright Andrew Biswell 2018

List of Books Withheld from Delivery by the General Post Office
Copyright International Anthony Burgess Foundation 1968

List of Anthony Burgess's Books Withheld from Delivery by the General Post Office of Malta in 1968
Copyright International Anthony Burgess Foundation 2018

Anthony Burgess Interview
Copyright Marie Said 1970

Obscenity & the Arts
Copyright International Anthony Burgess Foundation 2018

Photographs from Malta 1968–69 by Anthony & Liana Burgess
Copyright International Anthony Burgess Foundation 2018

Photographs from Malta 1983–89 by Liana Burgess
Copyright International Anthony Burgess Foundation 2018

Dirty Books & Laughing Stocks
Copyright Germaine Greer 2018

Transmogrifies
Copyright Adam Griffiths 2018

Feuerwerk
Copyright International Anthony Burgess Foundation 2018

Gladly My (Maltese George) Cross I'd Bear
Copyright International Anthony Burgess Foundation 1970

ALL RIGHTS RESERVED

Published by PARIAH PRESS 2018

PARIAH PRESS
www.pariahpress.com
pariah@pariahpress.com

British Library Cataloguing in Publication Data
Burgess, Anthony
Obscenity And The Arts

ISBN 978-0-9930378-6-3 paperback

Any edition of this book is sold subject to the condition that it shall not, by way of trade, be lent, resold, hired out, or otherwise disposed of, without the publishers' consent, in any form of binding other than that in which it is first published. No part of this publication may be reproduced, stored in a retrieval system, or transmitted in any form by any means, electronic, photocopying, mechanical or otherwise without prior permission of the copyright holder and publisher.

Cover art by Adam Griffiths
www.ra-bear.com

Set in Monotype Plantin
Typesetting by Geoff Read Arts
www.geoffread.com

Printed and bound by CPI Group (UK) Ltd

With thanks to: Will Carr, Graham Foster, Anna Edwards, Lisa Lorenz and Eilis Otway

• Contents •

The Context of Obscenity & the Arts Andrew Biswell	1
List of Books Withheld from Delivery by the General Post Office	33
List of Anthony Burgess's Books Withheld from Delivery by the General Post Office of Malta in 1968	35
Anthony Burgess Interview Marie Said	39
Obscenity & the Arts Anthony Burgess	49
Photographs from Malta 1968–70 Anthony & Liana Burgess	81
Photographs from Malta 1983-89 Liana Burgess	101
Dirty Books & Laughing Stocks Germaine Greer	111
Transmogrifies Adam Griffiths	129
Feuerwerk Anthony Burgess	145
Gladly My (Maltese George) Cross I'd Bear Anthony Burgess	153

The Context of
• Obscenity & the Arts •

Andrew Biswell

1: Burgess on pornography and obscenity

Anthony Burgess became an opponent of literary censorship when he was a schoolboy in Manchester in the 1920s and 1930s. In *Flame Into Being*, his book about the life and work of D.H. Lawrence, he recollects the climate of his early years, in which books such as *Lady Chatterley's Lover* and James Joyce's *Ulysses* were banned. 'We were inflamed with a desire to get hold of these books not merely because they were outlawed,' he wrote, 'but because the reactionary or popular press hammered at them so relentlessly.'[1]

Among the pro-censorship voices of the 1920s, none was louder than that of James Douglas, the editor of the *Sunday Express*. If the eleven-year-

---

1. Anthony Burgess, *Flame Into Being* (London: Heinemann, 1985), p. 2.

old Burgess had looked into his father's copy of the *Sunday Express* on 19 August 1928, he would have found the following review by Douglas of *The Well of Loneliness*, Radclyffe Hall's novel on a lesbian theme: 'I would rather give a healthy boy or a healthy girl a phial of prussic acid than this novel. Poison kills the body but moral poison kills the soul.'[2] The novel was suppressed and remained unavailable until 1946.

Like many of his contemporaries, Burgess was completely unpersuaded by the rhetoric of moral pollution circulated by journalists such as Douglas. As far as new literature was concerned, there was no higher recommendation than a damning review in the *Sunday Express*. The same newspaper greeted two of Aldous Huxley's early novels with reviews headlined 'Ordure and Blasphemy' and 'The Man Who Hates God.' Having read these inflammatory notices, Burgess knew it was his duty as a reader to seek out the complete works of Huxley with the shortest possible delay.

Burgess learned from his teenage years to associate literary modernism with the shock of the new, which was often called filth and obscenity by members of the older generation. At the age of seventeen he was lent a copy of James Joyce's *Ulysses* in the two-volume edition published in Paris by the Odyssey Press. Joyce's book, which was banned in Britain,

---

2. James Douglas, 'A Book That Must Be Suppressed' in *Sunday Express*, 19 August 1928. Quoted in Elisabeth Ladenson, *Dirt for Art's Sake: Books on Trial from Madame Bovary to Lolita* (Ithaca: Cornell University Press, 2007), p. 130.

America and Ireland, had been secretly imported by Burgess's history teacher at Xaverian College. He took it home to his stepmother's house, read it, and received the shock of his life—not from the four-letter words or the frank descriptions of defecation and masturbation, but from Joyce's bold innovations in literary technique and interior monologue. As an adult, Burgess often said that he had never recovered from this seismic first encounter. *Ulysses* immediately became his favourite novel, and it was, he said, the book against which he measured himself every time he sat down to write fiction.[3]

From the banning of Joyce and Lawrence in his youth, Burgess established a set of principles that he would reiterate whenever, in adult life, he was asked to put forward his views about censorship. Firstly, he believed that one of the main functions of literature was to be subversive, rather than to reassert or uphold the prevailing orthodoxies of the age. Secondly, he thought that if imaginative writers succeeded in causing offence among the moralistic, they could not be said to have betrayed their calling. His third principle was perhaps the most important: it was not the business of the state to tell people which books they should or should not read.

Burgess was born in 1917, and more than a hundred years later it is difficult for us to remember how repressive British society was during the first fifty years of his life. Theatrical censorship was enforced

3. See Burgess, 'Favourite Novel' in *Homage to Qwert Yuiop* (London: Hutchinson, 1986), pp. 429–31.

until 1968 through the Lord Chamberlain's Office, which vetted stage plays and allowed performances to take place only after any offending words—including overt references to suicide, abortion, homosexuality or sexual organs—had been deleted from the scripts. Bookshops ran the risk of police raids if they stocked items such as the engravings of Aubrey Beardsley. The public art galleries of London, Birmingham and Manchester were regularly visited by plain-clothes detectives on the lookout for potentially 'obscene' paintings, which could be confiscated and destroyed at the discretion of the police. In *Bound and Gagged*, his history of twentieth-century censorship, Alan Travis writes about the Home Office 'Blue Book', a list of more than four thousand books which had been subject to destruction orders made by Magistrates' Courts in the 1950s. This list, whose existence was always denied until extracts were published in 2001, was circulated to chief constables to help them work out which publications to seize and destroy. Among the banned novels were *Moll Flanders* by Daniel Defoe, *Memoirs of a Woman of Pleasure* by John Cleland, and *Intimacy* by Jean-Paul Sartre.[4]

One turning point was reached in 1960, when a jury at the Old Bailey acquitted Penguin Books, who had published *Lady Chatterley's Lover* in a cheap paperback edition and were subsequently prosecuted for obscenity. Yet the *Chatterley* trial

---

4. For more detail on the climate of censorship, see Alan Travis, *Bound and Gagged: A Secret History of Obscenity in Britain* (London: Profile, 2001).

was by no means the end of literary censorship in Britain. Although it was now possible for works such as Nabokov's *Lolita* to be published, there was widespread resistance to the next wave of the *avant-garde*, most prominently represented by American writers such as William S. Burroughs and Hubert Selby. When *Dead Fingers Talk*, a selection of writings by Burroughs, was published by John Calder in 1963, Edith Sitwell was one of several established figures who wrote letters of protest to the *Times Literary Supplement*. Burgess, who admired the experimental qualities of Burroughs's writing and later imitated them in *Enderby Outside*, immersed himself in this debate by sending a letter to the editor of the *TLS*, published on 2 January 1964. He made a more detailed defence of Burroughs when he reviewed his next next novel, *The Naked Lunch*, in the *Guardian* in November 1964:

> It's amazing how little is needed to slake the thirsts of the pornography-hounds, the prurient sniggerers, the protectors of public morals. From the title of Mr Burroughs's masterpiece they will be led to expect something illicitly agapoid, a sort of phallic Laocoön, and they will be disappointed. What they will find, on the other hand, is a palimpsest of obscenity so emetic that no amount of casuistry will be able to justify a charge of inflammation and corruption [...] The making of this particular work of art was part of an ineluctable vocation. It demands to be read. It will make the rest

> of the autumn's offerings look remarkably lumpish or puny.[5]

Burgess seemed to be in no doubt that Burroughs was a genuine literary artist whose writing had been misused by the people he dismissed as 'pornography-hounds.' In making this case, he must also have been aware that artistic or literary merit was one of the defences newly allowable in prosecutions brought under recent legislation. According to section 4 of the 1959 Obscene Publications Act, 'A person shall not be convicted of an offence [...] if it is proved that publication of the article in question is justified as being for the public good on the ground that it is in the interests of science, literature, art or learning, or of other objects of general concern.' In practice this meant that writers and publishers could ask critics and professors of English to give evidence about the literary merit of a work which had been alleged to be obscene. More generally, the 1959 Act reconfigured the role of critics and reviewers (of whom Burgess was among the most prominent from the early 1960s) by making it more important than ever that such aesthetic judgements should be clearly stated when a potentially controversial book was reviewed on first publication. Burgess himself was to be involved as an expert witness in one of the most famous obscenity cases of the 1960s. Some years later, he built a pivotal section of his novel, *Earthly Powers* (1980), around the fictional trial of a poet whose work is prosecuted for obscenity.

5. Burgess, 'On the End of Every Fork', *Guardian*, 20 November 1964, p. 9.

Burgess found himself embroiled with the fortunes of Hubert Selby's *Last Exit to Brooklyn* from the moment it was published in Britain. Reviewing the novel for the *Listener* on 20 January 1966, he predicted that this 'study of dreg-life in the sickest part of New York is bound to bring out the well-worn OBSCENITY banners.' *Last Exit* was one of six books under review that week, and Burgess found it less accomplished than other new novels by Kathrin Perultz, Alice Winter and Wendy Owen. He compared Selby's novel to *Love on the Dole* by Walter Greenwood, a depression-era novel about a working-class community in Salford, first published in 1933: 'How Dickensianly cosy and periphrastic it now seems, and how little the trials of the Salford oppressed in the thirties, as presented by Walter Greenwood, can engage our pity and anger. The trouble is that we've had a war since then.'[6]

The world of Selby's novel, Burgess went on to say, reeked of contemporary life, with its colourfully counter-cultural *dramatis personae* of pimps, queens and hip queers. Because Selby seemed to be presenting a journalistic account of a 'sick' neighbourhood in New York, which was narrated with a large amount of sympathy for the plight of the downtrodden, Burgess concluded that 'no book could well be less obscene.' Although this was only a brief review as part of a larger batch of new fiction, he did his best to make a case for the novel's redeeming qualities of social and literary importance.

6. Burgess, 'New Fiction', *Listener*, 20 January 1966, p. 109.

He must have been disappointed when members of parliament and the Attorney General took a different view. On 2 March 1966 Sir Charles Taylor, the Conservative MP for Eastbourne, spoke out against Selby in the House of Commons and demanded that his novel should be be prosecuted for obscenity. A private prosecution was brought in 1966 by Sir Cyril Black, the Conservative MP for Wimbledon. The Marlborough Street Magistrates' Court found the publishers, Calder and Boyars, guilty under section 2 of the Obscene Publications Act and referred the case to the Central Criminal Court. Although the publishers were found guilty of obscenity, this judgement was eventually overturned in the court of appeal in July 1968. Burgess gave evidence as a witness for the defence at both trials in 1966 and 1967, and shortly afterwards he wrote an account of the case for the *Spectator*. This was the first time that he published the arguments against censorship which later appeared in *Obscenity & the Arts* and his introduction to the 1968 post-trial edition of *Last Exit to Brooklyn*.[7]

Burgess divides art—although he is thinking primarily of writing—into three categories: aesthetic, didactic and pornographic. Literature, he claims, is purely aesthetic, because it depends for

---

7. Burgess, 'What Is Pornography?' in *Spectator*, 1 December 1967, pp. 683–4; reprinted in *Urgent Copy: Literary Studies* (London: Cape, 1968), pp. 254–7. For more detail on the Selby trial, see Frank Kermode, 'Obscenity and the Public Interest' in *Modern Essays* (London: Fontana, 1971), pp. 71–89.

its effects on verbal devices intended to provoke intellectual pleasure or (in the case of tragedy) to bring about catharsis. Literature, according to Burgess's definition, can never be 'kinetic' in the sense of trying to move readers in particular ways, which might include persuading them of a political case (the 'didactic') or inciting them to sexual fantasy (the 'pornographic'), which Burgess says will lead to 'onanistic discharge' (p. 255). Nevertheless, he is concerned to make the point that pornography 'is harmless so long as we do not corrupt our taste by mistaking it for literature.' Even if a book falls under suspicion of being obscene or pornographic, that should not be a reason to justify suppressing it. Readers must be free to make their own decisions.

Burgess is robust in his defence of writers and reputable publishers, and he questions whether members of the moralistic pro-censorship lobby are even qualified to understand the artworks they would ban:

> The best argument against external censorship by church or state is still Juvenal's: 'Quis custodiet ipsos custodes?' Why should a grocer-alderman consider himself qualified to prevent a student of Joyce from seeing the film of *Ulysses*? Why should a non-specialist and perhaps even only partly literate jury, directed by a judge untrained in aesthetics, prevent an honest enquirer from learning about the sexual mores of Brooklyn perverts? (p. 257)

If Burgess's *laissez-faire* attitude appears to be not especially contentious today, it's worth remembering that censorship of books, plays and films was very much a current issue in the late 1960s. This was partly because a pair of serial killers, Ian Brady and Myra Hindley, had been convicted in May 1966 for the abduction, torture and murder of three children. At the trial, it was suggested that Ian Brady, who had assembled a large library of erotic fiction, sado-masochistic novelettes and non-fiction books about Fascism and Nazism, had possibly been driven to his crimes as a result of consuming violent and sexually sadistic reading-matter.

The most vocal advocate of this position was the novelist Pamela Hansford Johnson, a one-time friend of Burgess and his first wife, to whom he'd dedicated his novel about Shakespeare's sexuality, *Nothing Like the Sun* (1964). Johnson had written about the trial of Brady and Hindley for a national newspaper, and the following year she tried to establish a connection between literature and murder in a polemical book, *On Iniquity* (1967).[8]

Johnson argued that killers such as Brady and Hindley lived in a post-Christian moral vacuum with no purpose, and that in such a society not all books should be available to all people. Although she stated that she did not wish to see clean-up campaigns or an extension of state censorship, she also said that if the price of a free press was the death of a

---

8. Pamela Hansford Johnson, *On Iniquity: Some Personal Reflections Arising Out of the Moors Murder Trial* (London: Macmillan, 1967).

child by torture, then that price was too high. In the concluding section of the book, Johnson quoted an article by Burgess about the French writer Louis-Ferdinand Céline, in which he'd written that 'a world in which everyone is both torturer and victim' was 'better than bourgeois death' (p. 140). This, said Johnson, indicated a rhetorical failure on Burgess's part to distinguish between real death and death as a metaphor.

Burgess replied to Johnson in 'What Is Pornography?', where he argued that Brady's reading of the Marquis de Sade had not created his instinct to commit sadistic acts. He wrote: 'Any book can be used as a pornographic instrument, even a great work of literature, if the mind that so uses it is off balance [...] Ban the Marquis de Sade and you will also have to ban the Bible' (p. 256). He predicted that there would be more violent crimes and murders if the 'reasonable catharsis of art' were taken away from ordinary readers. And the climate of censorship in Britain was enough to make everyone who wrote 'honest works of literature' feel uneasy. He feared that the next obscenity trial 'might be anyone's book', including his own (p. 257).

2: *Burgess and Maltese censorship*

Anthony Burgess arrived in Malta on 17 November 1968. The period of his residence covers five-and-a-half years, from 1968 to August 1974, but his house in Malta, which contained his manuscripts, his furniture and his private library, was not sold until 1998, five years after his death. It would be possible to argue that he never really left his residence at 168 Main Street in Lija, because his possessions remained there until the end of his life. Although his dealings with the Maltese government were not always harmonious, it is also the case that Malta occupies a central place in his novels and autobiographical writings. If Burgess had never lived there, we would have lost some of his best writing.

By 1968 he had published seventeen novels and a handful of translations and non-fiction books. Two important events happened in 1968 which changed the course of Burgess's life. His first wife died in March after a long period of illness. A few months later he met the woman who became his second wife, Liana Macellari, an Italian translator who was researching linguistics at Cambridge University, and they married in October. Liana had a four-year-old son called Paolo Andrea, later known as Andrew, and Burgess adopted this child and brought him up as his own son. Shortly afterwards they took the decision to leave England and begin a new life abroad. Malta was their first destination, and they bought an elegant eighteenth-century palazzo in Lija, having arrived by sea in November 1968.

Burgess recalls some of his earliest experiences of Malta in the second volume of his autobiography, *You've Had Your Time*, published in 1990:

> I took a taxi to the offices of the Electricity Board in Valletta and asked the ancient weary Maltese in charge if he would be good enough

> to turn on my supply. His response was: "The provision of electricity is a business that requires much lengthy negotiation. Why do you want electricity?" I told him. He said: "Let us consider the nature of electricity." [...] Back at the house in Lija I found a number of local Maltese, the Borg and Grima families, adjusting bare wires at great peril to themselves and even connecting a dusty telephone. An old man called Joseph Grima had already appointed himself gardener. A fat girl called Mary Borg said she was the maid. Naughty children coming home from school rang our doorbell. These I slapped.[9]

It's clear from this passage that Burgess's hatred of obstructive officials and functionaries is balanced by affection for his Maltese friends. Surviving letters to Burgess from his neighbours, now archived at the Burgess Foundation in Manchester, indicate that they also liked and respected him. Although it is sometimes said by hostile critics that he disliked Malta and insulted the people, it would be more accurate to say that it was the government of the day and its policies that he hated.

In some ways Burgess is unfair to the authorities in his writings about Malta. He complains that the government refused to give him a residence permit, but the papers in the archive confirm that Anthony and Liana Burgess both received their residence

9. Burgess, *You've Had Your Time* (London: Heinemann, 1990), p. 198.

documents on 27 November 1968. He also says that the government made trouble about his Bedford Dormobile (a kind of mobile home), and he says that they tried to confiscate it. The fact of the matter is that Burgess and Liana hadn't bothered to register their vehicle when they brought it to Malta, despite having received a number of polite letters asking them to do so, and they knowingly put themselves on the wrong side of the law. This refusal to follow simple regulations is entirely characteristic of Burgess and Liana's dealings with authority. All they had to do was fill in a form.

Another problem which confronted Burgess as a new immigrant was the difficulty of importing his large collection of books from England. Among his papers is a list of forty-seven books confiscated from Burgess's library by the General Post Office in 1968. He appealed against this decision and eventually four of the books were released, but the other forty-three volumes were driven under police escort to the hospital and incinerated. This was Burgess's first experience of Maltese censorship, and as a writer who had spoken out against the suppression of books in Britain, he took it very seriously.

One of the confiscated books was a Penguin paperback of D.H. Lawrence's *Lady Chatterley's Lover*. In his later book about Lawrence, Burgess shows himself to be an admirer of the novels, short stories, travel books and poetry. In 1985, to celebrate the centenary of Lawrence's birth, he composed *A Man Who Has Come Through*, a song cycle for chamber orchestra and male voice, based on four of Lawrence's poems. His favourite novels by Lawrence were *The Rainbow* and *Women in Love*, both of which had been banned on publication in Britain in the 1910s. Burgess's judgement on *Lady Chatterley's Lover* is that it is far from being his best book, and that it wasn't a good or successful novel. Nevertheless, he was certain that no book by Lawrence should be banned for obscenity. Writing about *Lady Chatterley*, he said:

> We know what goes on in the act of love, and those of us who are writers are in despair of ever finding verbal equivalents for the pain and pleasure of excitation fulfilled in 'venerean ecstasy' [...] Lawrence's apologia for his novel —'Apropos of Lady Chatterley's Lover'—is in some ways more entertaining than the book itself; it is certainly more humorous. He does not recommend that every sexually dissatisfied lady should run off with a randy gamekeeper, but he does locate 'the old blood-warmth of oneness and togetherness' in the lower social orders.[10]

Two novels by Kingsley Amis—*The Anti-Death League* and *Take a Girl Like You*—also appeared on the censor's list of items not to be admitted into Malta. Amis was an admirer and a friend of Burgess, a lecturer in English at Swansea University and later at Cambridge University, and a serious literary writer. Having been a fiery Communist in his youth, Amis became an outspoken Conservative in the

---

10. Burgess, *Flame Into Being*, pp. 182–184.

1960s, and later won the Booker Prize for Fiction in 1986. Although Amis had been accused from time to time, by critics such as Somerset Maugham and F.R. Leavis, of being a lower-class pornographer, to Burgess it seemed incomprehensible that his novels should be banned in Malta, or anywhere else. One of the other authors whose work was seized was Angela Carter, another close friend of Burgess, with whom he shared a literary agent, Deborah Rogers. It is more than likely that Carter's novel, *The Magic Toyshop* (1967), was judged to be unsuitable because the dust jacket copy promised a strong dose of feminism.

Three other books confiscated from Burgess's collection were *The Nun of Monza* by Mario Mazzucchelli (a novel about a nun who struggles to keep her vow of celibacy), *Seduce and Destroy* by James Eastwood (a spy thriller featuring a sexually uninhibited female assassin), and *Keep It Kinky* by Jonathan Clements, described on its back cover as 'the sex romp of the millennium'. The covers of all three books confirm that they are unsophisticated bodice-rippers, aimed at the more popular end of the market. *Keep It Kinky*, for example, is adorned with an illustration of a lusty couple apparently on the point of having sex in a graveyard. It is difficult to avoid the suspicion that the officials at the Post Office in Valletta were not reading these books, but simply making judgements based on their covers. Any book whose front cover promised nudity, adultery, prostitution, or even sex between married people, seems to have been confiscated.

The other reason why Burgess was enraged by the Maltese censors was that his own work was also banned in Malta. When his 1966 spy novel *Tremor of Intent* was translated into French under the title *Un Agent Qui Vous Veut du Bien*, the book was confiscated because the cover contained a photograph of a presumably naked woman under a bedsheet. When the same novel was translated into Danish with a more religious-sounding title, *Martyrernes Blod* (*The Blood of the Martyrs*), and a soberly religious cover image, it was approved by the censors with no difficulty. Burgess was quick to see the absurdity of the same book being, in its different editions, simultaneously banned and tolerated as suitable reading-matter for the pious Maltese. He decided it was time to make his views on censorship more widely known.

He was encouraged when he read in the newspapers about the new Censorship Reform Group formed by the Malta Library Association in May 1970. One of their key supporters was Marie Said, later known as Marie Benoit, a young Maltese journalist who had initiated a correspondence about book censorship with the Postmaster General and the Ministry of Trade at Cavalier House in Valletta. The invitation to give a lecture about obscenity was communicated from the Malta Library Association to Burgess via Marie Said, who had interviewed him for the *Sunday Times of Malta* shortly after he arrived. Once the date of the lecture had been fixed, the *Sunday Times* announced that Burgess would speak under the auspices of the Malta Library Association at the Science Lecture Theatre of the Royal University of Malta.[11] Burgess was quoted as saying: 'It's not up to the State to keep away the occasions of sin.' Members of the press and the general public were invited to attend. The title guaranteed that there would be a full house: *Obscenity & the Arts*.

When Burgess stood up to give his lecture at six o'clock on the evening of Wednesday 10 June 1970, he didn't know exactly what he was going to say. In his autobiography he claims that he prepared the text of his lecture carefully, but that seems not to have been the case. The published lecture, transcribed from a reel-to-reel audio tape and issued as a pamphlet by the Malta Library Association in 1973, shows every sign of having been improvised in the lecture room. Although the text indicates what an impressive public speaker Burgess could be, it lacks the polish and panache of the best of his literary essays.

The lecture itself is by now so entangled in controversy that it is difficult to see it for what it is— a great performance, in which Burgess demonstrates his powers of rhetoric and persuasion. Many people who have read the transcript are simply dazzled by the brilliance and energy of his speech. Looking more carefully, we can begin to see the extent to which Burgess depends for his effects on citing other works of literature. His argument about writing being either 'static' (meaning 'aesthetic') or 'kinetic' (meaning didactic or 'pornographical') is taken almost word for word from chapter 5 of

11. See 'Anthony Burgess Interviewed by Marie Said', *Sunday Times of Malta*, 7 June 1970, p. 18.

A Portrait of the Artist as a Young Man, in which Joyce's protagonist, Stephen Dedalus, talks to his university friends about his theory of aesthetics. From Dante's *Inferno* he quotes a line from the twenty-first Canto: 'Ed egli avea del cul fatto trombetta' ('He made a trumpet of his arse'), without letting on that the same quotation also appears in Joyce's *Ulysses,* on page 177 of the 1922 edition. It is characteristic of Burgess that he should look to Joyce, whose writings had also been banned, for assistance in building a case against literary censorship.

He also makes reference to more recent writing, specifically to a novel called *Mr Sammler's Planet* by Saul Bellow, newly published in 1970, from which he takes the episode in which Mr Sammler, a survivor of the Holocaust, is threatened by a pickpocket in New York. Burgess does not quote directly from Bellow's novel, but this is the passage he refers to: 'The black man had opened up his fly and taken out his penis. It was displayed to Sammler with great oval testicles, a large tan-and-purple uncircumcised thing—a tube, a snake; metallic hairs bristled at the thick base and the tip curled beyond the supporting, demonstrating hand, suggesting the fleshly mobility of an elephant's trunk, though the skin was somewhat iridescent rather than thick or rough. Over the forearm and fist that held him Sammler was required to gaze at this organ. No compulsion would have been necessary. He would in any case have looked.' Elsewhere in the lecture, Burgess trips himself up with his learned allusions. Speaking of the poet Virgil, he loftily refers to the 'known flame' which appears in Book IV of the *Aeneid* and assumes that his audience will know what he is talking about. But readers of the *Aeneid* will search in vain for this line in Book IV. In fact it appears in Book VIII, where Virgil is describing the male orgasm: 'At once he felt the usual flame; the familiar warmth passed into his marrow and ran through his melting frame.'

The other important reference is to his own work. At the end of his talk he mentions a passage from his 1966 novel *Tremor of Intent*, in which the protagonist, a spy called Denis Hillier, has an epic bout of sexual intercourse with a woman who turns out to be working for the enemy. Burgess describes having read this episode before an audience when he visited Vanderbilt University in Nashville, Tennessee, on 26 April 1967. He had forgotten, if he ever knew, that this reading was recorded, and the audio tape has recently been discovered in the university archives. The tape confirms that the reading was exactly as Burgess describes it: the response of the audience to this deliberately anti-erotic piece of writing was one of laughter.

Although Burgess is making a political speech with the aim of bringing about a change in the censorship laws, he still finds room for levity. In the middle of a rather dry discussion of the etymology of the word 'pornography', he breaks off to tell a joke:

> There was the young Scotsman who wished to marry his girlfriend but had no money and so, tortured by unseemly lust, he took her into the heather, and together, shamefully, they anticipated the marital rites. When it

> was over, Jenny said to Jock, 'Oh, Jock, I hope you will not think me a whore,' and Jock replied, 'Was there any talk of money when we started, lass?'

We can follow some of the responses to Burgess's lecture through the correspondence columns of the *Sunday Times of Malta* in the weeks that followed. On 14 June 1970 they printed seven letters, of which two were supportive of Burgess's position and five were against it. On 21 June there was a long and considered response from Paul Xuereb, one of Malta's foremost intellectuals, who suggested that Maltese Catholics were trying to outdo the Pope, who had abolished the Index of Prohibited Books several years earlier. Three more anti-Burgess letters appeared on 28 June, one of which, by Beryl Muscat of Sliema, accused Burgess of being a colonialist oppressor: 'It is no new thing for the local people to be bashed about by foreign (as well as local) aggressors; but in spite of this, what is best in Maltese life has remained constant and intact largely because it is well and truly hidden from the casually prying eye.' It was clear that Burgess had ignited a fierce debate—about book censorship and the influence of the Church in public life—which would not be resolved for many years.

In July 1970 Burgess was once again corresponding with the censors at the General Post Office. He wrote to ask for a complete list of banned books. They replied: 'With reference to your letter in which you requested a list of authors and books banned in Malta, I wish to inform you that it is impossible to supply you with such a list, as there are hundreds of authors whose books are banned.' Burgess wrote back and asked to see a list of books banned in 1969. Mr Aquiliana from the Ministry of Trade replied on 21 July 1970, enclosing a seven-page list of two hundred and seventy-five books which had been confiscated and destroyed the previous year. These included books about the Vietnam war, the James Bond novels by Ian Fleming, a book about the Marquis de Sade, *The Naked Ape* by Desmond Morris, plus various other works by D.H. Lawrence, Gore Vidal, Harold Robbins and Alberto Moravia. The censors had also confiscated books by Simone de Beauvoir (feminism, again), a book with 'contraception' in the title, and a number of literary novels by (for example) David Lodge, Margaret Forster, Howard Spring and Nicholas Monserrat. Thanks to the intervention of Burgess's friends at the Malta Library Association, the complete list of books suppressed in 1969 was published in the *Malta News* and the *Times of Malta*.

But that was very far from being the end of the story. On 25 June 1970 a lengthy attack on Burgess was published in the *Malta News* by somebody calling himself 'Paul Severini' (not his real name), under the headline 'The Style of Ingratitude'. The context of this article is that Burgess and his wife had visited a literary festival in Adelaide, where he had been interviewed on the subject of censorship and said that Malta was the most repressive country he'd ever lived in. Liana had intensified the insult by telling the same journalists: 'We stay at home when we're in Malta because it's less depressing than seeing life as it is.'

Paul Severini, who said that he was worried about Malta's reputation abroad, compared Burgess to a dangerous disease which threatened to infect the good people of Malta. He wrote: 'The Burgess rabies is now rampaging at our own doorstep. He was at it again in an interview on the subject of censorship which he gave to a Sunday paper recently. This time it was the prostitution racket allegedly run by Maltese in London and Sydney which swam into the ken of this remarkable man.' Severini ended his article thus: 'Mr Burgess's literary style is unknown to me. His style of ingratitude for the privileges he enjoys here as a sixpenny settler—however—prompts the reflection that in cases such as his, this phrase has a connotation that has nothing to do with income tax.' The implication that Burgess was a cheap and worthless hack wasn't altogether missing from what he had to say.

This was one of the most hostile pieces ever published about Burgess in his lifetime. It drew a strong response from the Maltese poet Edward Ellul, published in the Malta News on 9 July 1970. He wrote: 'All freedom-loving people in Malta must feel indebted to Anthony Burgess for speaking out loud. More power to his lungs. Our only hope of over-powering our intellectual jailers is to succeed in shaming them and holding them up to ridicule before the world, as they deserve.

We did not need Mr Burgess's fine perspicacity to notice that these islands are priest-ridden.'[12]

Burgess replied to Paul Severini in an unpublished letter, which was recently discovered, stamped and sealed in an envelope addressed to the editor of the *Malta News*, in the archive of the Burgess Foundation. The letter is dated 13 July 1970:

> It was a delight to read Mr Severini's diatribe against myself and my alleged ingratitude to Malta.
>
> I do not have to defend myself against anything, of course. I will say what I like about what I like wherever I like. This is the privilege of a free man, a concept perhaps not common in Malta, and it is the duty of a writer. If I see wrongs in Malta—and the repression of the enquiring intellect is a great wrong—I am not to be deflected from denouncing them because of the doubtful financial benefits of residing there.
>
> I have waited two years for a chance to state—uncensored—what I think of your disgracefully repressive approach to the arts and sciences. Now, it seems, thanks to the public discussion sparked by my recent statements, there are to be changes. Mr Severini will undoubtedly regret them.

12. Edward Ellul, 'Burgess Versus Bigots, Puritans and Pseudo-Patriots' in *Malta News,* 9 July 1970, p. 8.

It's worth asking why Burgess went to the trouble of writing this letter and then decided not to send it. Possibly he saw the favourable article by Edward Ellul and thought it was no longer necessary to respond to Severini in person. Or perhaps he was worried about causing further annoyance, in which case this would be a rare example of Burgess choosing the path of discretion and censoring himself.

His most public response to the Maltese authorities was contained in his novel *M/F*, written in Malta in 1970 and published the following year. *M/F* is almost totally neglected by readers today, but Burgess said that of all his novels it was the only one he was not displeased to have written. The book describes the adventures of a 20-year-old college dropout called Miles Faber who goes on a quest to discover the work of an outsider artist called Sib Legeru: a poet, painter, musician and novelist who in some respects resembles Burgess himself. Miles travels from New York to Castita, an imaginary island in the Caribbean. Burgess takes his revenge on the Maltese pro-censorship lobby by putting homosexuality, rape and incest at the centre of his story. In other words, *M/F* is exactly the kind of novel that the censors were working hard to prevent.

It is clear to any reader who knows the territory that Castita is closely modelled on Malta, and that Burgess must have written the novel out of his immediate experiences in 1970. What is the evidence for making this connection? The first clue is in the place-name. Castita means 'chastity' or 'celibacy', and the fictional island in the novel (like Malta in the 1960s) is a deeply Catholic place, subject to the influence of priests and archbishops. Religious processions are held in the streets and there is a statue which weeps blood—although this turns out to be a hoax perpetrated by pranksters. Partly it's the architecture that reveals Castita to be a thinly disguised version of Malta: in chapter 6 we're told that the island is famous for its great cathedral, which resembles the high baroque style of St John's Co-Cathedral in the centre of Valletta. Like Malta, Castita has recently been granted independence after a period of British rule. There are loud fireworks in the street during religious festivals (another Maltese tradition) and there is a local brandy called Azzopardi, which is one of the most common Maltese surnames.

One other feature of *M/F* is an invented language, which creates similar effects to the 'Nadsat' teenage slang Burgess had used earlier in *A Clockwork Orange*. Although 'Castitan' does not resemble Maltese in any way, it does reveal something of Burgess's versatility with language. He had been impressed by Vladimir Nabokov's novel *Pale Fire* (1962), which features a fictional language called 'Zemblan', which is said to be spoken in a 'distant northern land'. Zemblan is based on Swedish, with some elements of Russian. Castitan, by contrast, reveals itself to be a language which must have come out of southern Europe, since it is strongly indebted to Latin and Sicilian dialect. By creating a language with southern roots, Castitan holds up a mirror to *Pale Fire*, a novel which is itself fascinated by mirror-images. Through his use of neologisms and ludic fictional devices, Burgess found a coded way to respond to his Maltese hosts, although it is doubtful that many of them would have realised what he was up to at the time.

The next response to Burgess was more dramatic. Following a period of absence while he had been teaching for a year at City College New York, Burgess returned to Malta to discover that his house had been confiscated by the government. According to a requisition order dated 28 March 1974, the Housing Secretary ordered Burgess to deliver possession of the building and to hand over the keys within fourteen days. Burgess immediately reached for his lawyer, but at this point Liana Burgess decided that she no longer wanted to live in a place where such things could happen. There was an abiding suspicion that the confiscation of the house was connected to the publication of the text of his lecture the previous year. Burgess successfully appealed against the requisition order, but this episode marked the end of his period of residence in Malta. He rented out his house to the Australian High Commissioner and never lived there again. His final act was to take the story to the international newspapers, and it was reported on the front page of the *Guardian* on 10 April 1974. In the Malta chapters of *Earthly Powers* (1980), Burgess's character Kenneth Toomey also finds that his empty house has been confiscated by the Maltese government while he has been in hospital in Rome. The general portrait of Malta in this later novel is one of disillusionment, and it represents Burgess's final farewell to the island. Curiously, one of the novel's most admiring readers was the American ambassador to Malta, who sent Burgess a fan letter which led to a long correspondence.

Until the end of his life, Burgess went on writing essays against censorship, especially in relation to the James Kirkup blasphemy trial of 1977 and the Iranian *fatwa* issued against Salman Rushdie for his novel *The Satanic Verses* in 1989. When he was asked by the *New York Times* to sum up the case for liberalizing the censorship code for motion pictures in 1973, he took the opportunity to reflect on his own practice as a writer of 'permissive' literature:

> When I wrote a novel called *Inside Mr Enderby* in 1959, I had to make my foul-mouthed hero say 'For cough' (pronounced in the British was, this sounds obscene enough). When I came to *Enderby Outside*, the sequel, in 1967, there was no longer any need for euphemistic spellings. When I published the two novels together, in 1968, as *Enderby*, the reader was faced with pre-permissive and permissive versions of the same obscene language, all in the same book. I must confess I was happier with the euphemism, which at least required ingenuity.[13]

Despite these minor misgivings, Burgess ended his article with a clear statement of principle: 'The right of total explicitness must be there whenever the

---

13. Burgess, 'For Permissiveness, With Misgivings' in *New York Times*, 1 July 1973, pp. 19–20.

artist wants it, since he is his own best censor [...] The moral question is, of course, a lot of nonsense' (p. 20).

When he was in his seventies, Burgess revisited some of his earlier writing about unspeakable literature in a long satirical poem titled 'An Essay on Censorship', completed in April 1989. His immediate occasion for writing the poem was the Salman Rushdie affair of 1989. It remains unpublished, although he made some efforts to have it published in book form. In many ways this poem represents a mature distillation of the thinking that stands behind *Obscenity & the Arts*. A few lines will give the flavour of the whole:

> Authors, who eat and drink what they create,
> See the prescriptions of a foreign state
> As a mere aspect of a threat diffused
> Wherever the free-winging word is used.
> A book's unpublished lest it may offend;
> Published, its tenuous life is at an end
> While libel seems to mutter. Books are burned
> By activists whose muftis have not learned
> The truth of Heine's aphorism: 'Who
> Burns books will soon burn human beings too.'

The complete text of 'An Essay on Censorship', which exists only as a typescript, will be included in a new edition of Burgess's *Collected Poems*, to be published by Carcanet Press.

Today, thanks in no small part to the activities of the Malta Library Association and its supporters, Malta has become a more open society and censorship is looked back on as a historical phenomenon rather than a present reality. After a long debate, fiercely fought on both sides, theatrical censorship in Malta was finally revoked in 2016. Fifty years after Burgess first arrived in Malta, it is now possible to speak about him as having played a small but significant part in the literary history of the island. Gone are the days when he was regarded as a meddling outsider who went there looking to cause trouble.

With regard to the banning and burning of books in Malta—which of course included his own books—I think Burgess would have wanted to echo W.H. Auden, one of his favourite poets, who wrote, in *The Faber Book of Aphorisms*: 'Burning books do not lighten the darkness.'[14] Despite the passage of nearly fifty years, *Obscenity & the Arts* is as relevant to our own time as it was when Burgess first stood up to deliver his lecture in 1970. With great eloquence and panache, he reminds us that our fragile liberties might at any moment be revoked by the state, and that they are always worth defending.

---

14. *The Faber Book of Aphorisms*, ed. by W.H. Auden and Louis Kronenberger (London: Faber, 1962).

32

LIST OF BOOKS WITHHELD FROM DELIVERY

BY THE GENERAL POST OFFICE

No.	Title of book	Remarks
1.	The Anti-death League	Appeal upheld
2.	He and She	- do -
3.	Let Noon be Fair	- do -
4.	The Great Spy Race	- do -
5.	Between the Sheets	Appeal rejected
6.	Hotel Mamie Stover	- do -
7.	Lady Chatterley's Lover	- do -
8.	The Marriage Art	- do -
9.	Marriage, Sex and Society	- do -
10.	The Sordid Side of London	- do -
11.	Technique of Sex	No appeal was lodged
12.	Sabre-Tooth	- do -
13.	The Re-Assembled Man	- do -
14.	The Pumpken Eater	- do -
15.	Take a Girl Like You	- do -
16.	Virgin Soldiers	- do -
17.	File on a Missing Redhead	- do -
18.	Martha Crane	- do -
19.	The Bull Pen	- do -
20.	Ice of Grass	- do -
21.	What the Butler Saw	- do -
22.	Spring Fire	- do -
23.	Sex Trap	- do -
24.	To the Devil a Daughter	- do -
25.	The Satanist	- do -
26.	Unholy Crusade	- do -
27.	The Whipping Boy	- do -
28.	Orange Wednesday	- do -
29.	Benjamin	- do -
30.	The Magic Toyshop	- do -
31.	The Truth about the Pill	- do -
32.	The Best of Everything	- do -
33.	Tumult	- do -
34.	Dames Delight	- do -
35.	Memoirs of an Oxford Scholar	- do -
36.	Keep it Kinky	- do -
37.	The Conscripts	- do -
38.	The Psychology of Sex	- do -
39.	The Nun of Monza	- do -
40.	Notebook of Captain Georges	- do -
41.	Brothers in Arms	- do -
42.	Homosexuality	- do -
43.	Sex and Society	- do -
44.	Marital Breakdown	- do -
45.	Kimiko	- do -
46.	Seduce and Destroy	- do -
47.	The Corrida at San Feliu	- do -

H.R.Q. No. 6643

MTIA 1213/63

• List of Anthony Burgess's Books •
Withheld from Delivery
by the General Post Office of Malta in 1968

1. *The Anti-Death League* (1966) by Kingsley Amis
2. *He and She* (1960) by Edward Le Comte
3. *Let Noon be Fair* (1969) by Willard Motley
4. *The Great Spy Race* (1963) by Adam Diment
5. *Between the Sheets*
6. *Hotel Mamie Stover* (1963) by William Bradford Huie
7. *Lady Chatterley's Lover* (1928) by D.H. Lawrence
8. *The Marriage Art* (1961) by John E. Eichenlaub
9. *Marriage, Sex and Society* (1965) by Martin Arnold
10. *Sordid Side of London Town* (1967) by Norman Nash
11. *Technique of Sex* (1939) by Anthony Havil
12. *Sabre-Tooth* (1967) by Peter O'Donnell
13. *The Reassembled Man* (1964) by Herbert D. Kastle
14. *The Pumpkin Eater* (1962) by Penelope Mortimer
15. *Take a Girl Like You* (1960) by Kingsley Amis
16. *Virgin Soldiers* (1960) by Leslie Thomas
17. *File on a Missing Redhead* (1969) by Lou Cameron
18. *Martha Crane* (1954) by Charles Gorham
19. *The Bull Pen* (1969) by Alan Stuart Paterson
20. *Ice of Grass*
21. *What the Butler Saw* (1969) by Joe Orton
22. *Spring Fire* (1966) by Vin Packer
23. *Sex Trap* (1968) by Bill Turner
24. *To the Devil a Daughter* (1953) by Dennis Wheatley
25. *The Satanist* (1964) by Dennis Wheatley
26. *Unholy Crusade* (1967) by Dennis Wheatley
27. *The Whipping Boy* (1939) by Nicholas Monsarrat
28. *Orange Wednesday* (1967) by Leslie Thomas
29. *Mon Oncle Benjamin* (1842) by Claude Tillier

30. *The Magic Toyshop* (1967) by Angela Carter
31. *The Truth About the Pill* (1969)
32. *The Best of Everything* (1958) by Rona Jaffe
33. *Tumult* (1969) by Johannes Allen
34. *Dames' Delight* (1964) by Margaret Forster
35. *Memoirs of an Oxford Scholar* (1749) by John Cleland
36. *Keep it Kinky* (1969) by Jonathan Clements
37. *The Conscripts* (1968) by Walter Winward
38. *The Psychology of Sex* (1928) by Havelock Ellis
39. *The Nun of Monza* (1963) by Mario Mazzucchelli
40. *Notebook of Captain George*s (1966) by Jean Renoir
41. *Brothers in Arms* (1968) by Hans Helmut Kirst
42. *Homosexuality* (1955) by D.J. West
43. *Sex and Society* (1968) by Helena Wright
44. *Marital Breakdown* (1968) by Jack Dominian
45. *Kimiko and Other Japanese Sketches* by Lafacadio Hearn
46. *Seduce and Destroy* (1969) by James Eastwood
47. *The Corrida at San Feliu* (1967) by Paul Scott

• Anthony Burgess Interview •

Marie Said

Sunday Times of Malta, 7 June 1970

Anthony Burgess is one of the most talented and prolific novelists of our day. Although he regards criticism as a secondary activity he is also one of today's most perceptive and influential literary critics.

He was born in Manchester in 1917 and studied both music and languages at the University there. In 1940 he joined the British Army. He was determined to make his name primarily as a composer. It was not until he was in his late thirties that he started taking writing seriously enough to let it interfere with his musical composition. By then he had composed two symphonies, as well as sonatas, concertos for various instruments and popular songs.

After lecturing in England from 1946–1954 he went as senior education officer to Malaya where he wrote his first published books. After Malaya he went to Borneo as a lecturer but in 1959 he was invalided home with a suspected brain tumour. He was given a year to live so, in one year, wrote as many novels as he could. This warning proved groundless and Anthony Burgess now lives in Malta with his wife Liliana who is Italian. They have one son Andrea, who speaks fluent Maltese but not very good English!

The following is an interview I had with Anthony Burgess about a week ago.

Does the country you live in affect what you write?

Not greatly. I write novels, and these are made out of memory and imagination, not the immediate world outside.

Do you think the general atmosphere in Malta is conducive to writing?

In writing fiction I find one place as good as another. But there are certain kinds of writing that Malta doesn't help. Book criticism for instance. There have been too many instances of British and American journals of repute sending me books for review, and these same books being held up by the Post Office to be sniffed through by smut-hounds. The deadline passes, the job of reviewing has not been done, one's professional reputation suffers. There are certain periodicals which will never ask me to review books again. This is the fault of the Maltese state.

Which do you consider your most significant work?

The writer is never a good judge of his own books. The novel I am told, chiefly by the American academic world, is my best, is one I like very little —*A Clockwork Orange*. Stanley Kubrick is filming it at the moment. Although the book is a set text in American colleges and even religious seminaries, it means nothing in Malta, and I doubt if the film will ever be seen here. The book of mine I dislike least is *Enderby*.

You have done many things in the artistic field. You have composed music and you even paint. What do you like doing best? What is your greatest ambition?

I prefer composing music to writing prose—it's comparatively mindless. I've already composed, incidentally, an overture for the Manoel Orchestra, and I'm working on a symphonic sketch called *Ġiggifogu*. My big ambition is to write an opera based on James Joyce's *Ulysses*, that great Catholic literary monument.

You have 'harshly criticised' Malta on several occasions. Seeing that we have been under colonial rule for so long, don't you partly blame your own countrymen for a great many things which have been left undone, say, in the educational and cultural fields? Don't you think you are expecting far too much for such a small island?

Last question first. I don't think size has much to do with cultural achievement. Look at what ancient Athens did, as well as Elizabethan London. Blame colonialism by all means but remember that the British, unlike Napoleon, scrupulously refused to interfere with Maltese traditions and never tried to diminish the power of the Church. Malta has had its own destiny in its hands for many centuries. But by Malta I mean the ruling oligarchy, not the people. The people have always had a rough deal and they are still having it. Otherwise why so much emigration? They have never been encouraged to think for themselves. Their very language has been relegated to a minor place, while the oligarchs talked about art and politics in Italian or English. Who is to blame that Maltese has had an orthography for only a little over a century?

Surely Malta's paternalism has been a good thing—no drug addiction here, no sexual perversion, not much violence.

We can eradicate any public evil we wish most efficiently if we employ dictatorial methods. The secret of government, as of private morality, is to balance individual freedom of choice with what is considered to be a necessary apparatus of repression. Lead us not into temptation. But it's only to God that we pray; it's not up to the State to keep away the occasions of sin. There should not be any protection at all: it's up to us as individuals to engage temptation and try to conquer. That's what free will is about. Malta would try to do away with the concept of the Church Militant altogether and see this theocratic community as a trailer of the Church Triumphant. No fight against sin; no athletic struggle of the soul. Just the flabbiness of virtue achieved through sheer repression. If you can call such virtue virtue.

But you have to judge by results. Our 'protective' censorship system and mediaeval Catholicism make things safer for young minds and bodies.

Is any Catholic going to be so heretical as to suggest that ends justify means? God forbid. Incidentally, your Catholicism isn't 'mediaeval', it's typical of the eighteenth and nineteenth-century Papal States. Mediaeval Catholicism was creative not repressive. As for young Maltese being rendered safe from violence, pot and dirty books, that only applies in Malta. Get young Maltese abroad and they don't become notable for virtue. Wartime prostitution in London was run by the Maltese (some of whom, incidentally, nearly killed one of my best friends in Soho, W1, in 1946). Have you not heard of the Mediterranean Club in Sydney? Take off that chain of paternalism and the reaction in the direction of licence can be both murderous and suicidal.

As for censorship, am I expected to take seriously a system that held back one of the books I myself had written because it was in French—*ipso facto*, presumably, a dangerous language—and waved the same book through when it came out in Danish? The French title was *Un Agent Qui Vous Veut Du Bien* (meaning incidentally that the spy-hero ends up as a priest) but the Danish title was *Martyrernes Blod* —'Martyr's Blood', a holy title. Yet the two books were the same book. I can, admittedly, feel a little sympathy for censors who ban books with titles like

Topless Junkie, but none when they are solely concerned with killing the engagement of new ideas. Malta is the only country in the world that has banned books of one of its most distinguished residents—I mean Desmond Morris. Morris's fault? A scientific approach to human behaviour. And there are certain classics which are set books in the Catholic universities of America—*Candide*, for instance—still proscribed here.

The Maltese cannot yet discriminate and judge for themselves and the majority are not prepared to cope with a flood of permissive literature, films etc. What solution do you suggest for giving more intellectual freedom to a people traditionally not encouraged to think for themselves?

Are the Maltese different from any other people in the world? Are they not human beings? Give them what London or Rome already has—progressive cinema, the right to read books written and published in an honest spirit of enquiry as to the nature of man and society. Is Malta in greater need of protection than Rome? Or are Malta's faith and morality so shaky that they cannot resist the onslaught of new ideas and images of life? Christ came to bring not peace but a sword—meaning, I should have thought, the dialectic of human living through which the faith should be brightened and sharpened. As for a greater permissiveness in the provision of art and literature, people don't have to go to the library or the cinema if they don't wish. Nothing is being forced on anyone.

How do you think the Church has failed in Malta? What can it do to help build a society which is better equipped to cope with life in the modern world and at the same time retain a high sense of values?

I'd better say now that I'm a Catholic—one of a family that has suffered for its faith: I had an Elizabethan ancestor who was executed for refusing to accept the Queen as head of the Church. We've had to fight for Catholicism, which is more than the Maltese have had to do in the modern period, and I hold the faith precious. Moreover, as there's only one Catholic Church, I have a right to speak about the form of its manifestation in Malta. The Church in Malta is my Church as much as it is Archbishop Gonzi's. I think this about it: it tries to act for Caesar as well as God, despite Christ's insistence on the separateness of the two tributes. Indeed, it has tried to be Caesar. When a Church tries to build a theocratic state, embodying the individual will in the collective, then surely it's sinning in the direction of denying freedom of conscience. Theocracies are usually Calvinistic, which deny free will, recognise that predestination kills the significance—eschatologically speaking, anyway—of morals, and hence erect a system for the enforcement of the 'good'. It's strange to me to see Catholicism acting as though it were Calvinism.

Churches don't 'fail'. They're concerned with the Kingdom of Heaven, not the conduct of the secular state. The job of priests is primarily to administer the sacraments. Only they can do that. The job of teaching or learning Christian doctrine is the job of each one of us, lay or cleric. The Church in Malta

(I refuse to say 'the Maltese Church': there is no such thing) must stick to its task of preaching the Kingdom of Heaven and leave the Kingdom of Earth to the earthy politicians. But it's had so much secular power for so long that it will be reluctant to relinquish it. As long as this secular power is acquiesced in by the laity, and held by the clergy, Malta will remain a good place for young Maltese—with their curiosity, their intellectual honesty, their desire to see the world and make their own judgements on what they see—to get out of.

• Obscenity & the Arts •

Anthony Burgess

50

Preface to 2018 edition

In 1973 the Malta Library and Information Association (formerly the Malta Library Association) published what was in effect the first edition of Anthony Burgess's talk: *Obscenity & the Arts*. The result of an invitation by the Association to Mr. Burgess, then living in Malta, to deliver a talk at the University of Malta's Science Lecture Theatre —to what turned out to be a packed audience—in June 1970. The text of the address was recorded by the Association on magnetic tape, transcribed and finally edited by the author himself.

Carmel Borg
Secretary, MaLIA

Preface to the 1973 edition

In June 1970, the Malta Library Association invited Anthony Burgess to present his views, in the form of a public lecture, to its members and the interested public. The Science Lecture Theatre of the University of Malta was packed; the talk was duly delivered. The audience was fascinated: some were confused; a few were openly hostile: never had obscenity been analysed in public before!

The temptation to ask Mr Burgess for permission to publish the talk was too great to be resisted. It was generously granted. The magnetic tapes of the lectures were slowly but carefully turned into typescript, and the editing was done by the author himself. A young artist, Paul Sant Cassia, was approached about the cover and general design. The result is what you now hold. Our hope is that its contents may be inspiring and that its design may complement the contents.

Special thanks are due to Marie Said, who alerted the MLA about Mr Burgess.

MLA Publications Board

Foreword to the 1973 edition

I am safely assuming that very few people in Malta knew of the writings of Anthony Burgess until he started to write about *us*. I think our ignorance of him goes a long way towards proving his claim that because of censorship and associated reasons we are very far from keeping abreast of the outside world.

Burgess expresses his views with the authority of a distinguished novelist, who has also had a lifelong interest in serious music. In fact, he threatens us with a new symphonic work called *Ġiogdifogu* ('fireworks'), but I feel sure *his* version will be more melodic than it sounds!

Our Association considers it an essential part of its work to bring eminent literary figures of the present day to the notice of our still very limited reading public.

With the combination of such an inflammatory topic and his succinct and explosive style, I am sure that Anthony Burgess will understand me when I say that the reader is about to experience a slight 'tremor to his intent'.

Josie Montalo
Chairman, MLA

56

We are told a great deal by foreign periodicals that Malta is a delightful place. This, of course, we know for ourselves. But there is one flaw in the perfection of Malta, and that consists in the vast numbers of dirty books which prevail here in people's homes, in schools, and in universities.

There is one particular story, in one particular book, of which many copies are to be found here, that comes into my mind as an example of the kind of thing to which the Malta reading public is subjected. It's a story about a woman who hates a man and determines to take revenge on him. She arranges for her two sons to rape the married daughter of the man and, before raping her, to murder her husband. This they do, using the corpse of the husband as a pillow on which to execute the double rape. When the rape has been completed, they cut the girl's tongue out and cut off her hands so that she can neither utter nor write down the names of her assailants. But she takes a stick between her arms and writes their names on the sand. Her father sees the names, invites the two miscreants to his house, and there kills them. He bakes their flesh in a pie, making the flour for this pie by grinding up their bones. Then he invites the mother to a feast. She indulges in the most unmaternal cannibalism, he murders her, murders his own daughter who has brought shame on herself and shame on the house, and he murders himself.

That story is, as I said, to be found here in Malta. The fact that it was written by William Shakespeare (it is his *Titus Andronicus*) does not really excuse him, or exculpate the fact; but I and many authors like myself must wonder greatly sometimes what kind of standard of obscenity prevails on this island.

There are Dante reading circles, and every Englishman who reads Dante knows filthy lines like: *'Ed egli avea del cul fatto trombetta.'* There are presumably the works of Rabelais, that great doctor and luminary of the early Renaissance. What precisely is the standard prevailing on this island which decides that one book is dirty and another is not?

This is a question I ask academically. It is a question which is very near to me, very privy, because I am a writer and, believe it or not, no writer (certainly no novelist) deliberately writes obscenity any more than he deliberately perpetrates libel. He writes books to elucidate certain aspects of life, to entertain, but he also writes books to make money: it is his trade. And I have a friend, a writer, a distinguished English writer, Kingsley Amis, who cannot understand why two of his novels, which are of theological content, are banned on this island; whereas books, many banal, like *Lucky Jim*, are freely read. I cannot understand why certain books of mine are allowed on this island in English, but when they come out in French are immediately impounded by the Postal Authorities. So what I am trying to aim at is the establishment of some kind of rationale which will be helpful to us as writers and you as readers, and will elucidate for all of us the meaning of this very vague and subjective term 'obscenity'—and its ugly sister 'pornography'.

The term 'obscenity' is so subjective, so inflammatory, that apparently to attempt any kind of semantic elucidation is not easy. The word carries so much weight; it will do very well as an emotional counter but not as a semantic counter. What is an obscene thing? It is a thing which corrupts. What is a thing which corrupts? It is an obscene thing. The argument is circular. If we appeal to etymology and find out what the origin of the word was in Latin, we are given no help: *obscenitas, obscenus,* the terms have something to do with things of bad omen. The term is thrown around subjectively, as I say, but ultimately it always seems to have some connection with a particular mode of disgust—a disgust which derives from a particular zone of the human body or particular activities of the human body. In other words, we regard the lowlier, the purgative functions of the human body as necessary evils, things we must not talk about very much, and anything connected with these, thrown at us deliberately for some artistic, moral or immoral purpose, calls into being the term 'obscene'.

Let me give you a practical example: if I put a lump of human or animal ordure on your doorstep, I have probably performed an obscene act. The reason why I have performed this may not be particularly clear but you will undoubtedly interpret it as an insult, an expression of hate, or contempt, or the like. If, having deposited this lump of faeces on your doorstep I then ring the bell and ask for toilet paper, I am compounding obscenity with insolence. I would probably, if I found a lump of faeces, or a flask of urine placed on my door, or the contents of these vessels thrown into my letterbox, be justified in going to the police, saying an obscene act has been performed and I want to be protected from it. And, in the same way, I would feel that, if faeces and urine were scattered freely about the public streets, a kind of obscenity, a kind of insult to human dignity had been perpetrated. Again I would feel justified in calling on the civil authorities to do something about it. Push it further, push it to the point of artifaction and put up a poster on which (as on many New York posters, incidentally, at the present time) these lowly functions are depicted, then we are reaching gradually the sphere, not quite of art but certainly of communication through images—communication through conventional signs, or, if you like, iconic signs. I think I can begin with this: that the lowlier forms of purgation are regarded as disgusting. Why? Because they somehow detract from our dignity as human beings. We like to think of ourselves as progressing upwards and we want to forget our lowlier animal origins. If these are figuratively rubbed in our faces, we are immediately filled with disgust and filled with a sense that something ought to be done about it by our elected governors—the state, the police.

Now, there is a point here I must make because the purposeless, wanton insult offered to the community or the human individual by this kind of exhibition is itself perhaps disgusting, but it may be used for a purpose which is not at all disgusting. This is where many of our censors and many of our juries go wrong, because it is conceivable that in a period like, for instance, the eighteenth century, the Age of Reason, when men had forgotten their lowlier origins and even forgotten that they grew hair, shaving their hair off and putting wigs on instead, it was felt necessary by certain writers, certain highly moral writers, to remind men of their origins and to throw these purgative products in their faces for their own good. Dean Swift, Jonathan Swift, Dean of St Patrick's from Dublin, a clergyman, was a great, shall we say, combined scatophobe and scatophiliac. He both hated and was fascinated by faeces. He wrote poems in which the elegant toilette of a lady of fashion is suddenly qualified by a reference to her lowlier functions, to the adherence of the products of these functions to her own dresses. The poem about 'Chloe', if it is not banned in Malta, may be very well known to you. I will not quote all the relevant lines, because these are genuinely obscene, but the obscenity is there for a purpose. It is there for a strictly moral purpose, and not solely to disgust and not solely to titillate.

In *Gulliver's Travels*, you remember, Swift goes to great lengths to emphasise how disgusting an animal man is. He does this by blowing him up in the 'Voyage to Lilliput' section of the book, and by reducing him to a mere midget at the very end of the book. Here Gulliver lives among rational horses, which are clean animals. He identifies human beings with Yahoos, who, in equine opinion, are disgusting. After his stay, when he meets his own wife and family again after many years, he immediately faints with disgust at their smell. This is obscenity. This is genuine obscenity. This may seem to some of us to go too far, but one must give Swift the credit for not throwing these lowlier facts of our lives into our faces, but insinuating them in his miraculously rational prose for a high moral purpose.

What we tend to do nowadays is not to be quite as rational as people were in the eighteenth century, which could easily encompass this kind of writing. People like Dr Johnson may have had reservations about *Gulliver's Travels*, but nevertheless they would never have insisted the book be banned because of its obscene content. Nowadays, no matter what the obscene content is used for, the tendency is to regard the presence of obscenity at all, for whatever purpose, as automatically condemning a book to the flames.

This happened very recently in England with regard to an American book that is not on sale in Malta, and may not even have been heard of. It is a book by a lawyer called Selby, and the title of that book is *Last Exit to Brooklyn*. It is a series of stories dealing very compassionately, but very naturalistically indeed, with the lives of people living in the lower regions of New York State: the things that happen to them, the things they do, the aim being to arouse compassion through the depiction of obscenity in people's lives. Not only obscenity in the lowly sense to which I have already referred, but also obscenity in the deeper sense, sexual obscenity. When this book appeared in England there was a great fight to save it from the smut-hounds, people who put their snouts into the book, dug out the dirt, and then cried on heaven and the state to rid them of this incubus. The jury which sat on the book in England at the Old Bailey was not a jury which was accustomed to reading books, and it certainly was not a jury accustomed to reading *avant-garde* literature. They saw certain four-letter words and condemned the book as dirty. The book was then impounded until there was an appeal, headed by John Mortimer, the lawyer-playwright, who asked this very pertinent question: 'Well, what do you mean by obscenity? Let's come down to brass tacks. This case has cost a lot of money, it has cost the publishers more money than they can afford, it has cost the booksellers a lot of money. What does this term obscenity mean?' And then came the shibboleth. The obscene is that which corrupts. And what is that which corrupts? It is obscenity. Because of this circular argument it was admitted for the first time possibly in the whole history of English law that there was no objective definition of the term possible, and the book was freed. The book is now free, in America, in Europe (except for Malta), and is recognised as a book which, though frightening, though disgusting, is disgusting to the end that we should learn compassion, that we should understand that there are elements in the lives of human beings which must be brought into the open. There are diseases in the body politic which must in fact be cured.

I must dispel any impression you may have that I am on the side of the wholesale dissemination of obscenity for its own sake. There are magazines on sale, with whose names I will not sully this assembly by mentioning: it would be an obscene act, in fact, to do so. There are magazines which solely contain things which disgust the reader, without leading the reader to any sort of conclusion. I am not for the free dissemination of this kind of magazine, although I would say that, when this kind of magazine has come out, often enough it automatically kills itself as there are very, very few variations capable of being rung on the fundamental themes of obscenity. One magazine, whose title can be roughly translated as *Equine Ordure*, consists mostly of drawings of elderly people making love. This, of course, to many people is for some reason regarded as obscene. Sexual intercourse is right for the young and haired but not in order for the middle-aged and bald. It is something that we hear happens, but something which must never be depicted. This particular magazine makes a great play of depicting this kind of event for the purpose of disgusting. It is a magazine which also occasionally goes in the direction of a kind of obscenity we will come to later, but which I must mention briefly now, the obscenity of cruelty by depicting very finely drawn naked new-born children on the end of a bayonet. The implication, the unthought-out implication, being that this is the sort of world we have made. They mean nothing of the sort. They are merely meant to disgust. I am not for one moment suggesting that we allow a free traffic in this kind of pseudo-literature, but I am suggesting that we mustn't take fright at it, that it will automatically kill itself because of the limitation of changes able to be rung on the fundamental theme.

Now we move on from this kind of obscenity, which deals with the purgative processes of the human body and which seems to belittle man by removing him from the angelic orders and putting him among the bestial orders. We move from that by a kind of enharmonic chord to another kind of obscenity, which we can call pornographic obscenity. The enharmonic chord (you are all musicians here) is the chord which belongs equally to two keys remote from each other and enables us to change from one remote key to another. The enharmonic chord which moves us from faecal obscenity to pornography is, of course, the genitalia themselves.

God in his wisdom has decided that the organs we use for defecation and micturition are also the organs we use for generation. We cannot deny this: it is a fact and we cannot do anything about it except occasionally close our eyes to it. But it is because of this connection that automatically the sexual act, in many countries, has an association of the unclean attached to it. I think it was one of our great Church Fathers, Origen, who said, and forgive my Latin: *'nascimur inter faeces et urinam'*. Of course, he can naturally speak for himself, but he was greatly obsessed with this notion about our having been produced in the very area from which faecal matter and urine are produced. The association is long established, and the association is very hard to kill.

There is a novel, recently out in America, recently out in England, by a very eminent Jewish writer, Saul Bellow. The book (I don't think it is yet on sale here in Malta), though not obscene, presents obscene action which is rather significant. A Jewish exile from Europe, living in New York, sees on the bus a negro who is an expert pickpocket. The negro sees that he is seen; the seer is frightened, he runs away. The negro corners him in the hallway of his own apartment. The negro holds him against the wall, the negro undoes the fly of his trousers and takes out his genitalia and exhibits them and puts them back in again and goes away. He says nothing. But the Jewish protagonist of the novel is well aware that a kind of obscene act has been performed. What is the significance of the act? In what way is it a threat? There is nothing homosexual about it at all. It is merely an exhibition of something that is intended to disgust, which in fact does disgust. It is an obscene exhibition. Wherein lies the obscenity? Obviously, if we are going to think about this rationally, there is nothing obscene about the genitalia themselves, but the obscenity seems to lie in the mind of our Jewish hero (it seems to me) although this is not expressed explicitly in the exhibition of an aspect of man separated from the entity of man. The exhibition of genitalia reduces man from an entity into a mere machine capable of performing a particular function. It is, of course, well known that genitalia are not in themselves beautiful. Monkeys will frequently exhibit their genitalia in rage, meaning to put off a person they dislike. The association is not only with the function but also a kind of consternation that the genitalia in themselves are not beautiful, are ugly. This is why probably in most countries the genitalia are all stylized before they can be accepted in art. Stylized into phalli, into lingams, into Freudian symbols like wells, jewels, running water. In time, through this kind of stylization, the unsavoury and unseemly attributes of the plain physical genitalia can be expunged. There are many Indians, many Tamils, who carry names like 'Sundralingam' and 'Mahalingam'. *Mahalingam* means literally *big penis* and *Sundralingam* means *beautiful penis*, but the names do not really mean that. The term lingam has been cleansed of its totally, wholly physical denotation and has become almost a religious icon; it is that sort of association which is contained in the name.

Another kind of obscenity which seems to connect with the genitalia, with the act of reproduction, with the capacity for reproduction, with the capacity for fructification, with the capacity for copulation, divorced from the human entity, is to be found in a very curious book by Jean-Paul Sartre, one of his early books which is called *Nausée,* which means *Nausea.* The hero of this book, Roquentin, feels nausea when he sees, blooming in the square in the town where he lives, a chestnut tree. He is sick. The chestnut's blooming strikes him as being somehow an obscene act. It is, to use a Chinese term, a plethora of *yang*, a plethora of male principle, a plethora of the promise of fructification, a plethora of sex for its own sake. So you see in this region we have a kind of obscenity which is not quite yet pornography. We must now move to pornography proper where we have few problems in definition, partly because we have a very clear and straightforward etymology.

Pornography comes from two Greek words: *graphein*, to write or draw, and *porne*, meaning a prostitute. I gather that the words, in the roots from which *porne* is derived, the element of buying and selling is involved, but I do not think this buying and selling element applies when we use the term pornography today. I will, if I may, tell you a story in which the *porne* can be viewed under two angles. There was the young Scotsman who wished to marry his girlfriend but had no money and so, tortured by unseemly lust, he took her into the heather, and together, shamefully, they anticipated the marital rites. When it was over, Jenny said to Jock, 'Oh, Jock, I hope you will not think me a whore,' and Jock replied, 'Was there any talk of remuneration when we started, lass?'

It is not the remunerative factor we are concerned with. The *porne* in pornography—pornography in the simplest order—is the representation of a female sexual partner, whose name we do not know, whose mind we know nothing about and whose name and mind we are not greatly interested in. The representation of a sexual partner, whose desirability is not in doubt, is the fundamental pornograph, if I may coin that term. We have phonographs, iconographs, ideographs. Why not pornographs? A pornograph then can be found in the columns of the *Times of Malta*: any underwear advertisement will show a young lady, who is obviously a sexually desirable partner, whose name we do not know and whose mind we know nothing about, in whose fleshly endowments we are interested. This is a pornograph. It can be pushed further, of course, in the pages of magazines which are rarely found in Malta, like *Playboy*, where the ultimate simple pornograph is usually to be found with the odd tinge of exaggeration to spell out the sexuality of the pornograph.

Now, unfortunately we cannot get rid of pornographs even if we want to. I know that many of us when we go to London, going up and down the escalator in Piccadilly Circus tube station, see loads and loads of underwear advertisements which are pure pornographs. They represent desirable sexual partners. We do not attempt for one moment to get rid of them, and if such pornographs are in themselves compelling, how much more compelling must be the real thing. If we are going to talk about getting rid of pornographs, we must get rid of women. We cannot allow women to walk through the streets three-dimensionally, in mini-skirts, because they are desirable. We do not know their names, we do not go up and ask them who their favourite authors are or their favourite film directors. We are merely attracted. Presumably it is not wrong to be attracted, but we are, in the act of being attracted, encouraging the existence of three-dimensionally living pornographs on the streets of our cities. We can make these living pornographs less desirable as the Arabs do or, as I believe the leaders of the organisation here called MUSEUM do. We can cover them. We can cover them in *kabayas* and *yashmaks*, but anybody who has been in an Arab country will know that a woman in a *yashmak* or *kabaya* or *kaftan* can make with the ankles and make with the eyes, and there is no limit to what women can do with the least possible amount of equipment. I take it that we can accept for the moment that this kind of simple pornograph offends no one, although it seems to offend somebody, because we rarely see so-called 'girly' magazines on this island. There is no harm in girly magazines. They merely save us the trouble of using our imaginations. But I know what is at the back of the banners, the proscribers of such magazines. I will come to that in a moment.

May I in fact now suggest that the purpose for which these simple pornographs are intended, merely to excite minimally a kind of sexual emotion on the part of the male, is the germ out of which bigger kinds of pornography are made? Now, when we come to the sort of pornography which is called 'hard-core', the kind of pornography which not merely presents a desirable sexual partner, but presents this desirable sexual partner involved in the sexual act, then we come to a kind of pornography which is very different from the simple kind which I have already mentioned. We have come to a kind of pornography which has not solely the aim of sexual excitation, but the aim of a kind of solitary sexual fruition. The pornograph which depicts the act simply, or in some perverse form, some tortuous form, is there for a specific purpose. We cannot call it a social purpose; we can call it, if we like, a cathartic purpose. It is a purpose which young men and old men equally know all about. The lonely have sexual lives, but these sexual lives are solitary and take the form of masturbation. I am aware that I have hit on a subject which has to be viewed on an island like Malta under two lights: it can be viewed theologically, or it can be viewed civically. I must, I am afraid, leave the theological attitude to masturbation out of account for the moment, but when we have our discussion I hope this will come up. As far as the state is concerned, there is no harm in masturbation, hence there is no harm in the purveying of devices meant to excite sexual desire, and eventually procure the solitary sexual discharge. These do the state no harm, because indeed there is only one person involved with the pornograph. The thing happens behind shut doors, there is no attempt at imposing this act, which by its nature must be secret and solitary, on the rest of the public; and the act may be therapeutic, not only for the individual but for the state. It is conceivable that if sexual energy is discharged in this artificial way, it will not then flower into the various bizarre forms of violence which flourish in the cities of the West. I put it to you that it is possible, at least.

This kind of pornography, which is intended for this anti-social or, unsocial, or essentially solitary purpose, of course takes many and bizarre forms.

I have mentioned only the simplest kind, the kind you can see in action on the stage, in New York, even in London: the presentation of the sexual act, in all its glory, the fundamental function which men and women perform together, normally in private, made public. But then we move on to a much more bizarre, much more complicated, much more difficult to define, kind of pornography. We enter, in fact, a sort of country which has been called Pornotopia, where the only thought is lust and the only activity orgasm. We come to the engravings of the eighteenth century, we come to the works of the 'Divine Marquis', as he has been called. We come to the things which sometimes appear in odd bundles of eighteenth-century Anglican sermons at auction sales in England. We come to true hardcore pornography, and what do we say about it? We say about it that it is only there for the same purpose as the simple kind. It is there to effect a solitary orgasm. The Marquis de Sade himself is, of course, a clinical case. The works he wrote were devices, complex, bizarre, frightening, but they are for the same purpose as the simplest pornograph you can find in any shop in Charing Cross Road, to effect his own private orgasms, which were very stubborn to achieve and required the most bizarre and complicated machinery in order to effect them.

Now, what do we do about this? What does the state do about it? The state, in effect, should do little about it if pornography has no social significance. If the free sale of pornography merely promotes solitary acts of auto-eroticism, then pornography is doing no harm. But we come to another danger zone. Note how we are moving from a comparatively safe zone to a danger zone all the time, in which the name of the Marquis de Sade is a very relevant one. Some years ago in England there were some very horrible murders called the 'Moors Murders', in which a young man and a young woman tortured children, abused them sexually and then murdered them, and let their cries of pain and fear and, ultimately, their dying cries be recorded on tape with a background of pop music. Eventually they were caught and Pamela Hansford Johnson, the wife of Lord Snow, the novelist, wrote a book which came out of her daily attendance at the trial of the two murderers at the Chester Assizes. She had been brought up as a liberal, as indeed had her husband, and now she was, for the first time, it seems, in the face of genuine evil, theological evil. It is interesting to compare this with Jean-Paul Sartre, who, when he was a teacher, must have seen boys torturing flies and cutting birds' heads off with razor blades but never became aware of evil until the Occupation. The same thing happened to Pamela Snow. She must have known that evil existed, but now she became so strongly aware of it she felt compelled to write about it. She wrote a book which is full of heat and little light, and she made a great point of a statement made by the male defendant in court, when he was asked by the prosecuting counsel what books he had in his private library. He said he had a volume of the Marquis de Sade; it was in fact Marquis de Sade's *Justine*. The prosecuting counsel said: 'Is it conceivable that this influenced you in the way that you eventually went?' And he said: 'It is possible.' On that answer, Pamela Snow built up a thesis which says in effect that if we can save the life of only, merely, one innocent child, we should be prepared to curb totally what have long been regarded as the inalienable rights of the liberals, because if there is anything that is remotely inclined to send a potential murderer in the direction of potential murder, then we should be prepared to bring in the force of the State and have such a book proscribed. The argument is, somehow, lost because looking through the index of this book I discovered my own name there: 'BURGESS, Anthony', among other perverts and murderers. And I discovered that what she had done in effect was to accuse me of having made the statement that 'It is better to inflict death, cruelty, than to live a bourgeois life which is really only another name for death.' I had in fact published these words in a magazine article, but they were not *my* words; they were the words spoken by Céline, a writer who has sometimes been regarded as pornographic. This was a summing-up of his philosophy. She was so blinded by sweat and blood that she was unable to see the quotation marks.

Now, if she can do anything like this with one innocent, totally non-pornographic writer like myself, what does the rest of her argument mean? It certainly does not spring from a rational approach to the whole situation. Because if we take a rational approach, let us consider what books ought to be banned, what book can, even minimally, possibly arouse a sort of lustful desire to murder. Well, I remember when I was a small boy, I saw another small boy masturbating vigorously in front of a copy of the Holy Bible. It was one of those Victorian editions with the most lavish engravings. He was masturbating happily before an engraving of the *Dance Around the Golden Calf*. Rather an inflammatory picture, I must admit. What do we do? Ban illustrated Bibles? Then how about non-illustrated Bibles, as with the case in New York State of a man who murdered many children. When he was eventually found, he was asked why he murdered them, and he said he was a great reader of the Bible, and he was always most interested in the sacrifices perpetrated to make a sweet smell in the nostrils of the Lord by the patriarch Abraham. He was merely trying to do in his own life what a typical patriarch would have done. So with Haigh in England, who murdered many women and drank their blood. He said he was, from an early age, obsessed by the Sacrament of the Eucharist. Where do we go? We can in fact *not do* what Pamela Snow suggests. We can find nothing which, with somebody deranged, somebody potentially deranged or actually so, will not possibly drive them around the corner into the enactment of what previously is merely imagined.

Hamlet may persuade a young man to murder his uncle. All the tragedies written by the great Elizabethans may impel people to give poisoned flowers to their mistresses or crush their enemies to death with table-tops. There is no limit. If we are going to proscribe the presentation of sensationalism in literature, we are getting rid of a great deal of what we think is valuable literature. I am going to come very nearly to an end now, but I want to state, very much from my own point of view, where, in what region of values, condemnation of pornography can properly be made. I think the condemnation is more valid in the aesthetic rather than in the moral sphere, and I am being, I think, a good Thomist when I approach pornography in this way. Let me stick to my own sphere of writing for the moment. We can use words for three different purposes. We can use words to teach; in other words, we can use words in a didactic way. At the other end of the scale, we can use words to inflame; that is, we can use words for a pornographic purpose. In the middle we can use words statically; in other words, we can use words for an aesthetic or literary purpose. The literary function consists in arousing emotions, even indeed arousing physical desire, but only if the discharge of the emotion aroused is effected during the aesthetic rhythm of the work itself. This, of course, is as old as the hills, as old as Aristotle, the doctrine of catharsis, the purpose of drama, for instance, being to awaken passions which lie dormant in a civilised society, and having awakened them, to then discharge them in the process which Aristotle has called 'catharsis'. This is the purpose of all literature. I can read Tolstoy, I can read Shakespeare, I can read my own books. I can be excited, although I would not be with my own works. I can be emotionally aroused. But if, when I close the book, I am still emotionally aroused, I have not read a work of literature, I have probably read a pornographic work, or a didactic work. A didactic work, like say Samuel Smiles's *Self-Help* will impel me to discharge the meaning of the book. I close the book and then perform the act. If I buy a book on aerodynamics, I close the book and then do something about aerodynamics, I have dealt with a didactic work. With a book on ethics, the same thing applies. The significance of the book lies in what can be done when the book is closed. With a work of pornography, the same thing is true. The work of pornography can inflame and when the book is closed, the inflammation still exists, and has to be discharged. It may well be discharged in some totally non-sexual medium, such as public violence. But in the middle we have literature, we have works which arouse emotions only for their discharge within the rhythm of the work itself. It is a great shame when works of literature are confused with works of pornography.

There is a great deal of that happening at the moment in societies whose censorship has no clear rationale, and I would suggest that one of the first things our Maltese censors do is to consider this very simple *tri-partisé* division. Often they will seem to be condemning a piece of didactic writing because they think it is pornographic. They are moved, and they do not know what the nature of the motion is. This is precisely what happened during the *Last Exit to Brooklyn* trial in London. The jury was moved, but they did not recognise that the emotion they felt was compassion. They thought the emotion they felt was carnal, and they condemned the book. Pornography and didactic writing, ethics and pornography are far closer together than either is close to genuine literature.

If I may conclude with a personal reference, my own aim in writing is to avoid obscenity, and also to avoid didacticism, partly because I recognise the limitations of these two kinds of pseudo-art. We cannot do much with them. I recognise that when I write a novel, I must bring in the sexes because fiction is made out of the intercourse (sexual or otherwise) of men and women. Men and women marry in books and they go to bed together. I have never yet dealt in 'blow-to-blow' accounts of the sexual act. I am not interested. I am too much concerned with living my own marital life. I do not want to live it as it were vicariously. Indeed one finds that, overcome as we are nowadays by the state of 'blow-to-blow' fighting in the marriage bedroom, one is moved in ways that one does not expect, but such books as (say) Olivia Manning's *Balkan Trilogy*, which is about a married couple and contains only one reference to their going into their bedroom at all for a purpose other than sleeping. She says: 'They went into the bedroom and when they came out they made a cup of tea.' I find that, far more in some ways, inflammatory, than much of the hardcore pornography that is thrown at us. I find Virgil's reference in Book IV of the *Aeneid* to the 'known flame' far more appropriately inflammatory again than any 'blow-to-blow' account.

One must try to avoid, as far as one can, the raising of the reader's emotions, with no intention of discharging those emotions. Yet one cannot always win. I wrote a book, which has already been mentioned, rather cleverly, by your Chairman, *Tremor Of Intent* which is, in fact, on sale in a Penguin edition here in Malta, but it was held up at the Post Office—at least not allowed to be lent by me to anybody—because it came out in French, and French is *ipso facto* a suspicious language. The book, incidentally, is about a spy who became a priest. Simple as that. When the book came out in Danish called *Martyrernes Blod*, which means 'Martyr's Blood', it was almost whizzed through with an archiepiscopal blessing. You could smell the incense on it. This particular book contains at some length, a description of a sexual encounter which I had to bring in because it was mandatory, this being a spy novel, but my aim was to try and describe the sexual act in totally unerotic terms, in totally symbolic terms, in fact, so that the reader is not aware that the sexual act is going on unless he is skilled in reading symbolism. But when I was in an American university some years ago giving a lecture, a young man came up to me and said: 'Mr Burgess, I want to thank you very much for writing this book *Tremor Of Intent*, because my wife and I have been rather estranged sexually lately and I read this passage, the sexual passage, out to her and it put everything right. So thank you very much, Mr Burgess.'

It is evident that one cannot always win.

• Photographs from Malta •
1968–70

Anthony & Liana Burgess

1. Anthony Burgess (centre), Malta, 1970
   (Photographer: Liana Burgess)

2. Anthony Burgess (centre) and his son, Paolo Andrea, in the library of their home at 168 Main Street, Lija, 1970 (Photographer: Liana Burgess)

3. Anthony Burgess at work in his home at 168 Main Street, Lija, 1970
   (Photographer: Liana Burgess)

4 & 5. Liana Burgess in an unidentified restaurant en route to Malta, 1970
(Photographer: Anthony Burgess)

6. Paolo Andrea (Burgess's son) playing in the wreckage of a car, Lija, 1970
   (Photographer: Liana Burgess)

7. Paolo Andrea (Burgess's son) sitting in Burgess's Bedford Dormobile, Malta, 1970
   (Photographer: Liana Burgess)

8. Burgess standing in front of a bus, Lija, 1970
   (Photographer: Liana Burgess)

9. Burgess's Bedford Dormobile, Malta, 1970
   (Photographer: Liana Burgess)

10. Anthony Burgess walking along Triq Annibale Preca en route to his home at 168 Main Street, Lija, 1970 (Photographer: Liana Burgess)

• Photographs from Malta •
1983–89

Liana Burgess

1. Street scene, Malta, 1983
   (Photographer: Liana Burgess)

2. Beach scene, Malta, 1983
   (Photographer: Liana Burgess)

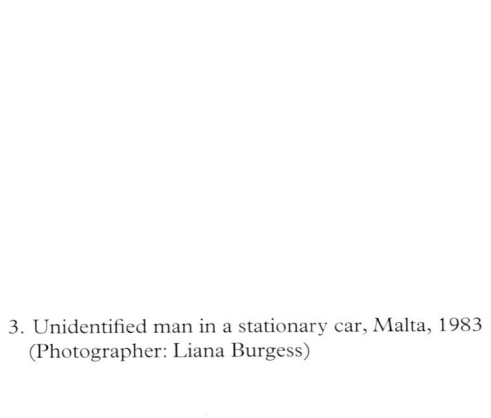

3. Unidentified man in a stationary car, Malta, 1983
   (Photographer: Liana Burgess)

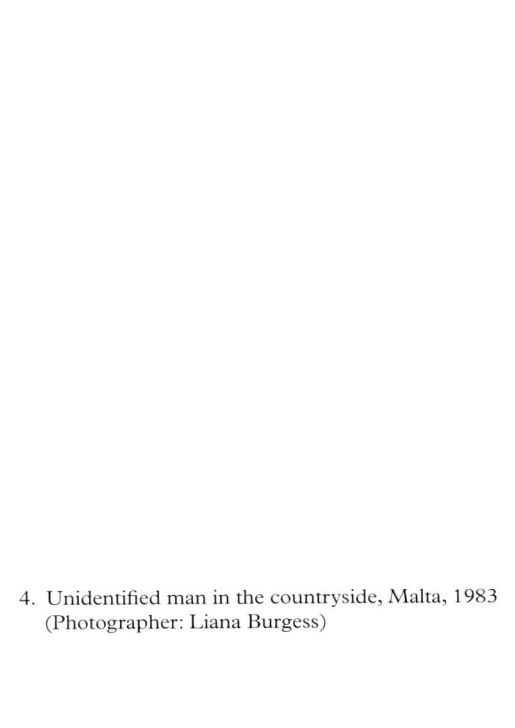

4. Unidentified man in the countryside, Malta, 1983
   (Photographer: Liana Burgess)

5. Front door of Anthony Burgess's home, 168 Main Street, Lija, c.1989
   (Photographer: Unknown)

• Dirty Books •
& Laughing Stocks

Germaine Greer

As Anthony Burgess, his new wife and son were travelling in their Dormobile in leisurely fashion across Europe towards their new house in Malta, back in London the counter-culture was enduring wholesale persecution. The Obscene Publications Squad regularly raided the offices of underground magazines and removed anything it felt justified in removing. The *International Times* had been prosecuted regularly since its inception; in 1970 the editors were charged with conspiracy to corrupt public morals by printing contact ads for homosexuals. The offices of *OZ* magazine had been raided several times before the issue of *Schoolkids OZ* in May 1970 provided the occasion to charge its editors with conspiracy to corrupt public morals, which carried a potential life sentence.

Academics like me who wrote for the underground press held themselves in readiness to be called as expert witnesses, to explain the uses of obscenity. We also studied how to avoid prosecution for using obscenity, and how to mount a legal defence. Burgess was not one of our number and had no connection whatsoever with the counter-culture which he can be considered to have parodied in *A Clockwork Orange*. Though he may have been severely incommoded by the refusal of the Maltese authorities to allow him access to certain publications, Burgess endured nothing remotely like the harassment and oppression that were the daily fare of British hippies and yippies throughout the 1960s and most of the 1970s. Only one of his ninety-odd books was pulped, but not for obscenity. As in the vast majority of cases, the first edition of *The Worm and the Ring* was pulped because of libel.

The Worm and the Ring was inspired by Burgess's time as a teacher at Banbury Grammar School in the 1950s. Many of the characters in the novel were recognisable as Burgess's erstwhile colleagues, including the school secretary Gwen Bustin who figures in the subplot as 'Alice'. According to Roger Lewis, Burgess's biographer, she was described as an 'incubus', 'a bit deranged... the sort of woman who should have got married ages ago', 'just pitiable'. She 'seemed to be suppressing an old maid's excitement', 'definitely unbalanced, the sort who might shout out dirty words under an anaesthetic'. Burgess portrays 'Alice' as desperate to seduce the school principal, which is probably what Bustin found too damaging to ignore. She sued for libel.

When Burgess knew her, Gwen Bustin was not yet fifty, and had already served as Banbury's mayor, deputy mayor and mayoress to a female mayor. She would hold the position of school secretary for her entire working life, which would seem to imply that she was very good at her job, which is not one that could be handled by anyone who appeared unbalanced. Miss Bustin's only crime would appear to have been that at fifty she was 'old.' Roger Lewis believes that Gwen Bustin 'rather proved that she was indeed a hysterical dried-up old duenna by reacting in the way she did—i.e. by hiring Colin Duncan QC to express her outrage in open court that she'd been portrayed in a book as a hysterical dried-up old duenna. One can only feel sorry for her.' One could also wonder what Lewis and his chums thought a duenna was.

Under the terms of Burgess's contract with Heinemann, he was liable for any damages, and the court could have well awarded all costs against him into the bargain. In *You've Had Your Time* Burgess described British jurors as 'notoriously against professional writers who wrote dirty books and were rich.' Burgess wrote to Bustin 'denying any malicious intent and apologising abjectly for any harm unintentionally done'. (Heinemann's lawyers must have torn their hair.) Bustin replied to Burgess's letter 'regretting' what Burgess had done and 'the whole situation'. According to Burgess,

> Heinemann sent her a hundred pounds. The case never came to court. But *The Worm and the Ring* joined the immeasurable mound

of pulped books. This was no way to earn a living.

At the same time as Burgess was complaining about the pulping of his book, Francis King was having to sell his house to raise money to pay the legal costs of defending a suit brought by Tom Skeffington-Lodge whom he caricatured as Dame Winifred Harcourt in his novel *A Domestic Animal*. That too was duly pulped. Like Burgess, King had been silly enough to send a written apology to Skeffington-Lodge. British libel law remains a principal limitation on freedom of speech, not just in Britain but across the world and into cyberspace.

Burgess's use of the word 'dirty' requires some unpacking. As a writer of reviews for the *Yorkshire Post*, he chose to draw attention to *Inside Mr Enderby*, the first book of his Enderby series written under the pseudonym Joseph Kell, by calling it 'a dirty book'.

> This is, in many ways, a dirty book. It is full of bowel-blasts and flatulent borborygms, emetic meals ('thin but over-savoury stews', Enderby calls them) and halitosis. It may well make some people sick, and those with tender stomachs are advised to let it alone. It turns sex, religion, the State into a series of laughing-stocks. The book itself is a laughing-stock.

When his masters at the *Yorkshire Post* realised that Joseph Kell was one of Burgess's pen names, and this was no more than a back-handed attempt to promote the book, they sacked him. This odd little episode encapsulates an embedded contradiction in Burgess's personality, where an urge to shock warred with his determination to commandeer the moral high ground. We could perhaps conclude that Burgess was suffering from Portnoy's complaint as defined by Philip Roth: 'A disorder in which strongly felt ethical and altruistic impulses are perpetually warring with extreme sexual longings, often of a perverse nature.' Burgess is by turns orthodox and perverse. The combination serves him ill in the case of his greatest success, *A Clockwork Orange*, which was published the year before *Inside Mr Enderby*. Burgess may have conceived it as a mere *jeu d'esprit*, 'knocked off for money in three weeks' but it was to have a life of its own, especially after Stanley Kubrick turned it into an iconic movie. A writer can make clear his detachment and contempt for his characters and their lifestyle, but a film can display no such subtlety. Once Burgess's characters had been cast, designed, dressed, expertly lit, as expertly shot and projected on the big screen, they had become glamorous, that is, spellbinding. The result, according to the British police, was copy-cat violence.

Several rapes and murders were linked to the film during its original British run. A 17-year-old Dutch girl was raped in Lancashire by a gang chanting *Singin' in the Rain*, and a judge who sentenced a 16-year-old boy who had beaten a younger child while wearing Alex's uniform of white overalls, black bowler hat and combat boots spoke of the 'horrible trend which has been inspired by this wretched film'.

In 1974 Kubrick would withdraw the film which would not be seen in British cinemas again until after his death. In 1985, Burgess wrote in *Flame into Being,* his book on D. H. Lawrence:

> The book I am best known for, or only known for, is a novel I am prepared to repudiate: written a quarter of a century ago, a *jeu d'esprit* knocked off for money in three weeks, it became known as the raw material for a film which seemed to glorify sex and violence. The film made it easy for readers of the book to misunderstand what it was about, and the misunderstanding will pursue me until I die. I should not have written the book because of this danger of misinterpretation, and the same may be said of Lawrence and *Lady Chatterley's Lover.*

Burgess blames Kubrick's film for what he sees as the misunderstanding of his book, which if he had had better control of the writing would have supplied the corrective to Kubrick's version, which happens to be the better crafted and the more charismatic. Typically, though Burgess might have been prepared to repudiate *A Clockwork Orange,* he didn't actually do so. Nor did he give Warner Brothers their money back.

In 1970 Heinemann produced a revised and expurgated edition of *The Worm and the Ring* to which, although he did not himself carry out the revision, Burgess must have agreed. It may have been this high-handed treatment of his work that prompted him to give a lecture on obscenity and the arts so soon after his arrival in Malta. Accounts of the event appear to have been influenced by Burgess's mythomania. His audience was not 'an audience of priests', or even 'three hundred Catholic nuns and priests'; there was no mass exodus; he was listened to with interest to the end and went off for drinks with members of his audience afterward. Par for the course.

Burgess begins his oration with an account of the kind of dirty book that was to be found in Malta, by summarising the plot of *Titus Andronicus*. He chooses to call Shakespeare's play a 'story', which it clearly is not and to credit Shakespeare with inventing it, which he did not. The play's full title is *The Most Lamentable Romaine Tragedie of Titus Andronicus*; the dreadful acts which constitute the plot are not what was seen in Shakespeare's theatre any more than they would have been in Seneca's theatre. The object of the exercise is to arouse pity and terror. Burgess's roping in of Shakespeare is a deliberate sophistry, which hardly connects with the next samples of obscenity, being references to farting in Dante and 'the works of Rabelais'.

> What precisely is the standard prevailing on this island which decides that one book is dirty and another is not? This is a question that I ask academically. It is a question that is very near to me, very privy, because I am a writer and, believe it not not, no writer (certainly no novelist) deliberately writes obscenity any more than he perpetrates libel.

This is simply wrong. There is a whole vast and multifarious genre of writing which has as its aim to provoke revulsion. Jonathan Swift did not write 'A Beautiful Young Nymph Going to Bed' or 'The Lady's Dressing Room' by accident. As an expert witness in obscenity cases I have struggled to explain to judges that tragic satire in particular exists to disgust. (After hours of explaining Juvenal and tragic satire to one judge, I was graciously informed that his honour did not read French.) When Burgess states with confidence that 'an obscene thing' is a 'thing which corrupts', he accepts the hypothesis of the censors and throws away his argument. Obscenity can and often does function as aversion therapy.

Obscenity can be adapted to almost any use. It can be agonising or hilarious. In the seventies Peter Cook and Dudley Moore developed a series of dialogues between 'Derek and Clive': their medium is pure, unadulterated obscenity, elevated to a level where it becomes fantastic, visionary, and almost purely abstract. It embodies a deliberate flouting of the undermeaning of the Latin compound, 'unfit to be seen'. Obscenity consists in transgressive display. Again we could consult Burgess's great contemporary, Philip Roth. To explain why he couched *Portnoy's Complaint* within a psychoanalytic session, he explained that this would allow him to bring into the narrative:

> The sort of intimate, shameful detail, and coarse, abusive language that [...] in another fictional environment would have struck

[him] as pornographic, exhibitionistic, and
nothing but obscene.

Exhibitionism is the aspect of obscenity that Burgess
simply did not get. His examples of obscenity do
not work because there is no element of offensive
display.

> ... if I put a lump of human or animal ordure
> on your doorstep, I have probably performed
> an obscene act.

If I am a herdsman milking a goat on your
doorstep, as was common in Malta until well
after 1970, and my goat defecates, the event is
not just not obscene, it is entirely insignificant.
Boy babies in the Mediterranean used to be
toilet trained by being put into split pants; at
first they simply squatted where they were, and
then they learnt to squat in an appropriate place.
Nobody considered the display of infant genitals
or of misplaced excrement as obscene. As an
adult your responsibility was to perform your
necessary functions unseen. Being seen about
an activity that was private is only obscene if
you mean it to be witnessed. When Romanian
women accused of stealing from passengers on
the London Underground were detained by the
transport police, they would put a hand up under
their voluminous skirts, wipe it over their genitals
(or so the police believed) and threaten to smear
the palm across the policemen's faces. This was
obscene theatre and it worked. The transport
police were paralysed with horror.

It is at this point that Burgess refers to a magazine which, out of consideration for his audience he calls *'Equine Ordure'*. This is none other than *Horseshit: An Offensive Review,* of which four numbers only were published by brothers Thomas and Robert Dunker, in Hermosa Beach, California between 1965 and 1968. It featured anti-military propaganda of a highly offensive character, including the example Burgess chooses, an image finely drawn by Robert Dunker of a naked, new-born baby impaled on a bayonet. The rest of his description of the review as consisting of images of elderly people 'making love' is, as far as I can ascertain, a case of mistaken identity. For no good reason Burgess denies the Dunkers their own obvious purpose which was to intensify revulsion about the Vietnam War.

Having disposed of this exemplum of the vast publishing activity occasioned by opposition to the war in Vietnam by dubbing it 'pseudo-literature', Burgess rambles on:

> ...the lowlier functions of purgation are regarded as disgusting. Why? Because they somehow detract from our dignity as human beings. We like to think of ourselves as progressing upwards and we want to forget our lowlier animal origins.

Mammals do more shitting than the lower orders do. One of the lowliest of all creatures is the antlion, which does without an anus. It defecates only once in its lifecycle as it emerges from the pupa. The only way for any mammal to refrain from defecating is to die. What Burgess appears neither to know or even suspect is that many animals are keen to dissociate themselves from their excrement, probably because its smell is apt to alert predators to their presence. Cats carefully bury their faeces and can be easily trained to use something like a shower outlet, where it is flushed away. Dog owners walking behind their pets hail the awaited turd with joy, knowing that they have simply to scoop the poop and head home. Burgess talks of the inappropriateness of shit being scattered about the streets, apparently oblivious to the amount of dogs' faeces to be stepped in on London streets in the 1970s. The truth is that we agree to ignore faeces; Pepys wrote about his motions, as did Smollett, but most authors in any era do not bother to tell you who went to the lavatory or when.

Part of what prevents Burgess from engaging with his subject is his resolute heterosexuality. He moves from a lame discussion of obscenity to an even less penetrating examination of pornography. He knows that the Greek root *porne* means prostitute, and then assumes that it involves the representation of a 'female sexual partner'. In fact it involves the representation of any fuckable creature for the titillation of a potential user of the same. As advertising it is part of merchandising. Burgess treats underwear advertisements on the Underground as if they are displays of the same kind though their function is to sell the underwear and not sex with the model. Such advertisements are, as nearly all porn is not, designed to appeal to women. Burgess's susceptibility to such advertising might be an indicator of a fetish of his own. His accounts of his actual sexual activity are entirely untrustworthy. He remained a Catholic, was apparently monogamous, endured long periods of sexual inactivity and probably, guiltily, masturbated. This he may have thought of as corruption or, as mother church has it, pollution.

The so-called sexual revolution of the 1970s was not one; what happened was that censorship was gradually relaxed. In Britain the process began with the Obscene Publications Act of 1959, which held that a work that possessed 'literary merit' could escape conviction for perceived obscenity. Penguin Books famously put the new law to the test by publishing *Lady Chatterley's Lover* by D. H. Lawrence. A succession of literary figures asserted the book's literary merit, unmoved apparently by obvious examples of Lawrence's racism and sexism or by the fact, unsuspected by most of the people involved, that the climax of the intimacy between Connie and Mellors is an episode of anal intercourse. The prosecution did not produce expert witnesses of the same calibre, and the jury found the publishers not guilty. *Lady Chatterley's Lover* went on to sell three million copies. Over the next twenty years prosecutions on the grounds of obscenity were gradually understood to be counter-productive.

Publishing may have been liberated, but sexuality had not. Coming on to the scene as a pornographer in 1971, when I joined the editorial board of *Suck* magazine, I soon found that current versions of our sexual culture were male-centred, and the dominant fantasy was sadistic. In an effort to break the mould I suggested that the editorial board pose for nude portraits, rather than exploiting younger, prettier, poorer, female people. When it came to myself, I had no option but to produce an image that could not be ripped off by commercial wank mags, and so I lay on my back, brought my ankles up over my head and looked at the lens through my knees. As I wrote about it much later:

> Face, pubes and anus framed by vast buttocks, nothing decorative about it. Nothing sexy about it either. Confrontation was the name of the game. Not so much kiss my arse as kiss my arsehole—a different matter entirely.

Suck magazine... ran the picture full page but not as a cover, because the image could never have been exposed on a bookstall anywhere, not even in permissive Holland.

Part of the object was to bring a sudden end to the piecemeal revelation of the female body; first the nipple began to be seen, then pubic hair, then split beaver, and ultimately my deliberately grotesque version of the utterly, undeniably obscene. The appearance of the picture on page 3 marked the end of my association with the paper. My male colleagues never exposed themselves naked as I thought we had agreed, but chose to print my contribution as a full broadsheet page with an appended signature cut from a letter. I had not been consulted and would not have consented to the use of the image in this form. I had made the mistake of thinking my male colleagues and I were on the same side. We weren't. *Suck* was meant to be the antidote to the New York magazine *Screw* subtitled 'Jerk-off Entertainment for Men', but it was the same old same old. Pornography is still jerk-off fodder for men, but with the invention of the Internet it has snowballed to become thirty per cent of all the data transferred.

The fact that the potential user of pornographic material is always assumed to be male is an issue for men to address. They are the people who embark on their sexual life using pornography for solitary gratification, who respond to a stereotyped stimulus that will not be provided by another human being, and who pay for their consumption of commercial stimuli. Their actual sex partners, if they ever acquire any, will have needs of their own, as pornography does not, and the man reared on porn will be ill-prepared to imagine or respond to them. If it is true that thirty per cent of all data transferred across the Internet is porn, it may be that we have already entered on an era of virtual sexual activity which is far less stressful, less time-consuming and more reliable than actual sexual intercourse. We can only wonder what might have happened if Burgess had run his thoughts on pornography past Philip Larkin, whose reputation has hardly benefited from the knowledge that after his death his solicitor had to remove from his home two large cardboard boxes of pornographic magazines, some of them featuring violence and bondage.

Pornography is no more a feminist issue than is domestic violence; the victims of both are far from exclusively female. Nobody knows what proportion of the vast array of pornography is made for a gay clientele; it may well be more than half but we do not find men protesting against the proliferation of porn and demanding to 'take back the night'. Pornography comes in a vast array of genres; it may be gonzo, POV, genderqueer or none of the above; it may feature infants, children, animals, transsexuals, on-face ejaculation, celebrities, fisting, shemales, anal sex, threesomes, amputees, torture, necrophilia, watersports, deep sodomy, autoasphyxiation; the putative consumer, straight or gay, is always male. Women use it, to be sure, but it is not designed for them.

In our semantics the individual who is fucked is—fucked. As long as that word contains its sadistic colouring, pornography will continue to degrade everyone who is associated with it. Obscenity however is a different matter; it took Mikhail Bakhtin to explain the many functions of obscenity; his works did not become widely known or fully understood in Britain until the late 1990s, too late for Burgess.

• Transmogrifies •

A series of visual studies that seek to re-contextualise source photography disinterred from the International Anthony Burgess Foundation archive; tangential to the processes of censorship employed by the General Post Office of Malta during the period: 1968–1974.

Adam Griffiths

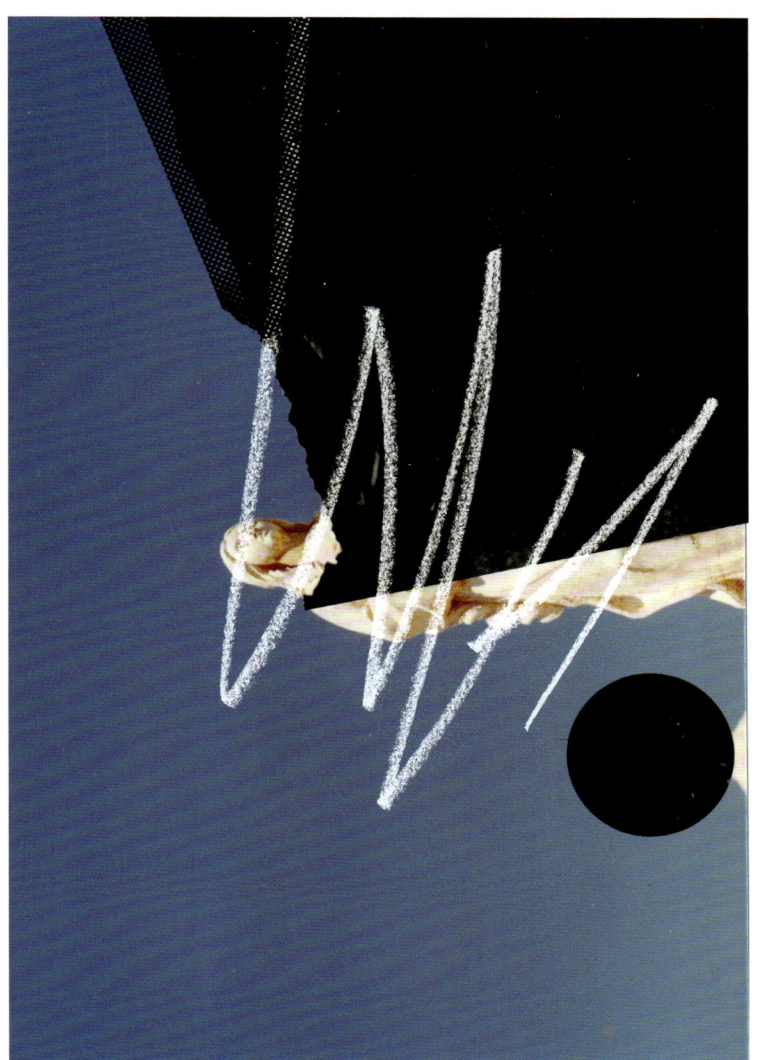

• Feuerwerk •

Piece for solo piano, 1969

Anthony Burgess

Feuerwerk

Molto Vivo

• Gladly My (Maltese George) •
  Cross I'd Bear

Anthony Burgess

Punch, 10 June 1970

Everybody is entitled to dodge paying confiscatory income tax if he can (and British income tax is a great glory of confiscatoriality, confiscatorialness —I'm too lazy, in this Mediterranean sun, to look up the right word). Authors, I think, have a duty to dodge paying it, knowing how little the State cares about the balancing of the many lean years and the few fat ones. But the ignorant and ill-disposed always assume that, when a British author runs away (scuttles away, sneaks away) to a sunny sterling-area tax haven, it is solely because he has become rich and unpatriotic. Not so, really. The author in Britain just waits till things add up. Add the lack of daylight (my sight is deteriorating) to the lack of subject-matter (Britain has little that isn't purely parochial) to the price of alcohol and tobacco. Fill up to a spumous overflow with death duties and tax on the living. Drink it all down and, drunk, convince yourself that the world needs your writing. Then scuttle or sneak or run.

Why Malta? Because it's not easy to get out of the sterling area and Malta is in it. So, of course, are Gibraltar, Cyprus, India, Australia, parts of the Caribbean. There are various arguments against those, however: too small, too big, too far away, too exotic. Malta is right in the middle of Mediterranean civilisation and a short sleep's distance from London. The Maltese speak English as well as their own Arabic dialect. They sell draught Bass and Senior Service. Their income tax for expatriate residents is sixpence in the pound.

Ill-disposed Maltese call us the sixpenny settlers, but they don't know the whole story. There is no reciprocal tax arrangement between Malta and the various non-British countries where one's books are published—America, for instance. The succession duty situation is (though there's talk of changing it) pretty dangerous. A British settler recently died and left £100,000. His widow had to pay both United Kingdom and Maltese death duties—a total of £120,000. One can't afford to die just yet.

The curious thing is that, no matter how little direct tax one may pay, one's bank balance never really seems to improve. Import duties are high here. Electricity and water aren't cheap. Things break down and are difficult and costly to repair.

Doctors and dentists have to be paid. One can't afford (three and six for twenty untipped) not to smoke more.

What kind of life does one get for one's money? Malta hates adverse criticism so I'll be wholly laudatory (*Times of Malta* please copy). There's plenty of sun, and the sea is no more stiff with effluent than at Southend. There are few trees and hardly any birds. What birds there are the Maltese are uneasy at seeing on the wing, so they have to be brought down to the cage or the pot. This, of course, is wholly in order, since the lesser creation is here for man's use and refreshment. Besides, as a lady pointed out in the *Times of Malta* only last week, fox-hunting and bull-fighting are far more cruel than bird-shooting, since foxes and bulls are so much bigger than birds.

Talking about meat, the posh new hotels tend to pre-empt the better varieties and cuts, but Maltese cheese is very good and bland and Maltese bread has a wonderful tough crust. Sometimes one can buy fish. You can get drunk and silly on the local wine, made from raisins, at eighteenpence the bottle. The garlic, being so good, is not always easy to come by. It taps you rather than assaults you, and you can eat a whole knob like an apple. So nutriment is no worry here.

Malta is a bulwark of Catholic Christianity, which is heartening to see in a world that is so rapidly jettisoning its spiritual values. Maltese Catholicism is wonderfully conservative, except that the Mass is said in the vernacular and God is addressed as

Allah, and priests go around in swishing skirts like (Graham Greene's simile) mediaeval warhorses. Morality must be protected, which is right, and the uncovering of inflammatory female flesh is, except on the beach, forbidden by secular law. Nobody likes to be inflamed, so this is to be wholly approved. The doctrine of socialism is essentially materialistic, so members of the Labour Party were excommunicated some years ago. They were reinstated lately, perhaps on the orders of Rome, which is known to be a giddy and Godless town, what with the Via Veneto and Fellini and Visconti. Many of us Tories feel that the Archbishop should have put up more of a fight on behalf of Catholic logic.

But censorship, which is in the secular arm's hands, goes on, to every serious person's satisfaction. A translation of a book of mine was confiscated because it had a girl on the cover and was entitled *Un Agent Qui Vous Veut Du Bien*—French, a highly suspect language. When the same book came out in Danish it was called *Martyrernes Blod*—or Martyr's Blood—and whizzed through to me almost with an archiepiscopal blessing. Again I think this was right, since the Danish title is more appropriate to the content of the book than the French one.

Newspapers like the *Daily Mirror* and the *Sunday Times* and the *Observer* are examined regularly for dirt, and sometimes bits are cut out with scissors or rolled over with an inkroller. British newspapers, of course, are known to be dirty, because of Swinging London and pot and so on. The new movement in the cinema has no friends in Malta, so films like

Bloody Hand of Vendetta and *Dracula Lives Again* are seen in place of *Midnight Cowboy* and *Easy Rider*. This again is in order, since people go to the cinema with their children for entertainment, and not to see the dirty world which they see enough of every day. Not, of course, that they really see it in Malta.

There are fine churches, cathedrals really (at least one to every village), built by the Knights of Malta, who were eventually got rid of and quite right, as they were mostly foreigners. And there are Roman remains. There are also lots of parties, duly reported in the *Sunday Times of Malta*. The Noble Mrs Gzira is there, also Freddy Xemxija and Mary Qattus. There is a lot of bridge too, but sometimes there is time for a bit of serious conversation—about books, for instance, such as the latest of Dennis Wheatley, Denise Robbins or Barbara Cartland. It is good to see people buying books occasionally. I have never seen anybody buying these authors in towns like New York or San Francisco, which are swinging and pot-smoking.

A lot of people are coming to Malta these days, and letters are frequently published in the local press from visitors who, cold now in Stoke-on-Trent, look back nostalgically on their fortnight of sterling sun and thank Malta for so theologically arranging it. They also praise the local people, who are so nice and unspoilt, with none of the acquisitive vices of affluence that so disfigure the British working class. How charming, too, to see them content with their homely nourishing diet of spaghetti pie and potatoes with bread on the side, varied with the odd sandwich of tomato conserva, since what you've never had you never miss. We would come back to Malta next year, only the Government has raised the tourist allowance and we are told they speak quite good English in Mallorca. (Captious letters are not published, since there's enough nastiness in the world without adding to it.)

The real advantage of Malta to the expatriate writer is that there's little to distract him from writing. I mean, there are belly dancers and drag artists at the posh hotels, but that's an aspect of the swinging pot-smoking civilisation that one is trying to get away from. There are no provocative films or TV programmes to churn up the mind, and none of that Dublin-style literary bibulousness which makes you say 'I'm writing a darling book' and then blurt it all out, making the writing superogatory. You're on your own on this double-cross island (Maltese and George), helping to keep civilisation going. And if Malta isn't particularly interested in your efforts, that's because she's got enough civilisation of her own. She'll be the first to tell you that.

• A Word on the Words •

The main body text is typeset in Monotype Plantin, a precursor and prime influencer of the later Times New Roman. During the period covered by this work a great many of Anthony Burgess's books were set in MT Plantin.

Chapter titles are typeset in Monotype Sabon. A font developed in Germany, shortly before Anthony Burgess arrived upon Maltese shores. We found Sabon to be the closest match to the letter punches used in a number of documents authored by Mikiel Anton Vassalli in the 1790s in his scientific standardization of the Maltese language. Vassalli himself was exiled from Malta on numerous occasions.

"This is a pleasing *stuffat*, as they may or may not say on Malta. Burgess was nothing if not dependable—dependably brilliant, dependably self-mythologising, dependably sorry for himself... As ever the genius and the charlatan are so interlinked that you don't know which is the host and which is the parasite. Not that it matters. He was, is, and always will be the greatest English writer of the second half of the twentieth century. This is a useful and stimulating addition to the oeuvre, and timely given the hypersensitivity of every group to criticism from without."
Jonathan Meades - author of *Museum Without Walls, An Encyclopedia of Myself* and writer-presenter of *Ben Building: Mussolini, Monuments and Modernism*

"There has always been a vocal minority that knows how the rest of us should live, what we should see, read and think. Its barks often rally a pack that makes it hard to hear voices against it. In Anthony Burgess the twentieth century had a strong answering voice, and this new work is its backstage pass. It couldn't be more timely, read it now—those barks are on the rise again."
DBC Pierre - author of *Vernon God Little* and *Release the Bats*

"In an age when freedom of expression is under grave threat, if not from the State then from fear engendered by social media pressure groups, this book, featuring Burgess's trenchant opposition to censorship, is timely and important. Writers should never surrender!"
D.M. Thomas - author of *The White Hotel* and the *Russian Nights* tetralogy

"Anthony Burgess had a very sane view of sex in literature. He believed that censorship was an evil. He knew that sometimes people looking for excitement might find literature. He approved of all kinds of excitement. When I met him and Liana they were madly in love. And probably madly in lust. They both seemed so alive. This is always

"This is an excellent and significant book. It documents Anthony Burgess's anti-censorship protest back in 1970 against the Maltese authorities' ban on importing books which ludicrously caught titles such as Desmond Morris's *The Naked Ape* and Ian Fleming's James Bond novels. It may seem to us now like some Lilliputian struggle from another age in which a much-esteemed novelist is punished by exile. But it was an echo of a much larger struggle that had taken place in Britain only a few years before."

Alan Travis - home affairs editor, *The Guardian* and author of *Bound & Gagged: A Secret History of Obscenity in Britain*

"Coming from a country which in the past suffered under a system of censorship that was at once pernicious, crippling and absurd, I welcome this account of a little-known but fascinating passage in the life of one of the finest English writers of the twentieth century. Anthony Burgess was an unremitting defender of artistic freedom, as *Obscenity & the Arts* amply attests."

John Banville - author of *The Sea* and *The Untouchable*

"A vivid reminder of the liveliness of Anthony Burgess's brain and his confrontational refusal to accept any kind of suppression or censorship."

Desmond Morris - author of *The Naked Ape* and *The Soccer Tribe*

"For a time in the 70s Anthony B. bestrode our world like the colossus he was—in real life, in fiction, in drinking, in courage and in his endless capacity to love and laugh. What a wise and lovely and courageous man he was, and how much his wisdom is missed. It took a great film maker, Kubrick, to remind us in *A Clockwork Orange* just how wise he was, because I'm not too sure we celebrated it as we should have done at the time."

Tony Palmer - director of *All My Loving* and *Bird on a Wire*, author of *The Trials of Oz* inspiring! Anthony knew that every human culture had celebrated Eros. He understood that our contemporary erotic lives were stunted. He totally surprised me by understanding Eros in my work better than any other writer. He wrote an essay on *Fanny: Being the True Adventures of Fanny Hackabout-Jones* that absolutely delighted me. I miss him and his wonderful work. I recommend *Nothing like the Sun* to everyone I know. He committed the ultimate novel about Shakespeare and he very much inspired my *Serenissima*—A novel in which I imagine that Shakespeare visited Venice during the plague year. He has left us a great treasury of wonderful books."

Erica Jong - author of *Fear of Flying* and *The Devil at Large: Erica Jong on Henry Miller*

"Burgess seems to have been physically incapable of writing a dull sentence, no matter how unpromising his subject, and his brief but impassioned account of the obscene and the pornographic continues to instruct and delight. Liberally coated with the fruits of Burgess's vast reading—he refers, among others, to Swift, Shakespeare, Dante, Sartre and Celine—it is also charmingly idiosyncratic. Which other English author would reach for the term 'enharmonic chord' to clarify his drift? Hats off to Pariah for bringing this treat back into print."

Kevin Jackson - author of *Constellation of Genius: 1922–Modernism Year One* and editor of *Schrader on Schrader*

"The story of Anthony Burgess's censorship tribulations in Malta is a powerful tale that needs to be told, and this book tells it brilliantly. In a world of electronic communication, where new forms of *Wiki*-censorship hide behind such labels as 'moderating', his reflections on the semantics of obscenity and pornography make his message as relevant now as it ever was."

David Crystal - author of *By Hook or By Crook: A Journey in Search of English* and *The Oxford Dictionary of Original Shakespearean Pronunciation*

"Anthony Burgess, a lifelong member of the awkward squad, is well served by Pariah Press's edition of *Obscenity & the Arts,* his 1970 lecture on obscenity delivered in censorious Malta. It is framed by an interesting essay on the cultural context by his biographer, Professor Andrew Biswell, and a lively critique by Dr Germaine Greer, herself involved in counter-cultural debates on pornography around the same time. Some poignant photographs and the author's handwritten score for a fiery piano piece add flavour to a book which no devotee of Burgess should miss."
  Nicholas Rankin - author of *Defending the Rock: How Gibraltar Defeated Hitler* and former chief producer at BBC World Service

"A must-read. Burgess provocatively, questionably and contradictorily engages with issues of censorship and definitions of obscenity and pornography, while Germaine Greer's argumentative and informed counterpoint provides a retrospective and wider frame for his argument. The outcome is a challenging debate on a time delay, across locations and gender perspectives, on a topic that still kindles controversy."
  Carla Sassi - author of *The International Companion to Scottish Poetry* and consulting editor for the *International Literature Quarterly*

"In 1970, author and composer Anthony Burgess mounted an impassioned case against censorship two years after forty-three books from his personal collection were burned by the Maltese government. His speech to the Malta Library Association displays humour, grit, and all the erudition we've come to expect from Manchester's most notable polymath."
  Christine Lee Gengaro - author of *Listening to Stanley Kubrick* and *Experiencing: Chopin*

"This book may contain material that will cause upset and offence to some people. Good. Some people need to be upset and offended. In an age when trigger warnings and no-platforming are in danger of becoming the norm, we need books like this as reminders of why hard won freedom of speech is essential to a free society. Along with the excellent contextualising essays by Biswell and Greer, Burgess gives us a clear reminder as to why the censorship of art is always wrong, and every arts and humanities tutor in our universities should place this on their students' core reading list."

Michael Paraskos—author of *Rabbitman* and *In Search of Sixpence*

"Pariah's rescue of Anthony Burgess's Malta speech is a timely excavation of social and literary history, a perfect opportunity to encounter or re-encounter Burgess's splendid provocations, and an elegant piece of publishing in itself. It is also a reminder of how certain battles persist, and how we'd best remain bold and irritated enough to win them."

Jonathan Lethem - author of *Motherless Brooklyn* and *The Fortress of Solitude*

"This book proves, once again, what we already know: there's no end to Anthony Burgess. Lucky us, he keeps coming back. *Obscenity & the Arts* reads and delights as some sort of non-fictional out-take/bonus track to his autobiographies and, in a very playful yet serious way, to his masterpiece (one of many): *Earthly Powers*. Here, again, the odyssey of an Artist with a capital A surrounded and besieged by many lowercase fools. Malta was not a moveable feast for Burgess but, in these pages, becomes a frantic celebration for his followers and fans. In the end, Burgess leaves the scene of the crime and trial but his life and work justly, and victoriously, remain. *Obscenity & the Arts* is also especially enlightening in this new puritanical dark age of supposed tech-liberation—yet ultimately clockwork-controlling-Ludovico-censoring irreal reality."

Rodrigo Fresán - author of *The Invented Part* and *The Bottom of the Sky*

"As a citizen of what was once a Soviet-bloc country (Hungary, that is) where state censorship was rendered superfluous by self-censorship, I used to find solace in surreptitiously reading Anthony Burgess's wonderfully outspoken novels. As a member of a largely Westernised academic community in East-Central Europe, I still look to the same works for hope and encouragement. That *Obscenity & the Arts* has seen print after lying dormant for decades holds out the promise that freedom of speech may yet be more than a mirage in a world that never was and never will be."

Ákos István Farkas - author of *Will's Son and Jake's Peer* and *The Magyar Tigris*

"This is a fascinating book with real literary and historical impact. Accompanied by new images of the writer and his family in Malta and thoughtful critical contributions from Andrew Biswell and Germaine Greer, this publication illuminates the circumstances of an intellectual conflict in a particular time and place, but provides important context to the wider issue of literary censorship in the twentieth century. We are struck once again with the eloquence of Burgess's rhetoric, the imagination of his arguments, and his skilful blend of moral and logical justification for artistic freedom. In 1993 the world lost a fine mind and pen, but this welcome coda serves to remind us of the treasures Anthony Burgess bequeathed to us. "

Simon Rennie - author of *Little Machines* and *The Poetry of Earnest Jones: Myth, Song and the 'Mighty Mind'*